PRESIDENT'S MALARIA INITIATIVE

Democratic Republic of the Congo

Malaria Operational Plan FY 2015

ABBREVIATIONS AND ACRONYMS

ACT	Artemisinin-based combination therapy
AL	Artemether-lumefantrine
ANC	Antenatal clinic
AS-AQ	Artesunate-amodiaquine
BCC	Behavior change communication
CCM	Country coordinating mechanism
CDC	Centers for Disease Control and Prevention
CDCS	Country Development and Cooperation Strategy
CNOS	National Council of Health Non-Governmental Organizations
C-IMCI	Community Integrated Management of Childhood Illness
DDT	Dichlorodiphenyltrichloroethane
DFID	U.K. Department for International Development
DHS	Demographic and Health Survey
DPM	Department of Pharmacies, Medicines, and Traditional Medicine
DRC	Democratic Republic of the Congo
FY	Fiscal Year
GDRC	Government of the Democratic Republic of the Congo
Global Fund	Global Fund to Fight AIDS, Tuberculosis, and Malaria
GHI	Global Health Initiative
iCCM	Integrated community case management
IMaD	Improved Malaria Diagnosis
INRB	*Institut National de Recherches Biomédicales*
IPTp	Intermittent preventive treatment for pregnant women
IRS	Indoor residual spraying
ITN	Insecticide-treated mosquito net
KOICA	Korean International Agency for Development
M&E	Monitoring and evaluation
MICS	Multiple Indicator Cluster Survey
MIS	Malaria Indicator Survey
MOH	Ministry of Health
MOP	Malaria Operational Plan
MSH/IHP	Management Sciences for Health/ Integrated Heath Project
NGO	Non-governmental organization
NMCP	National Malaria Control Program
PARSS	*Projet d'Appui à la Réhabilitation du Secteur de la Santé*
PHC	Primary health care
PMI	President's Malaria Initiative
PMURR	*Projet Multisectoriel d'Urgence pour la Réhabilitation et la Reconstruction*
PNDS	*Plan National de Développement Sanitaire*
RBM	Roll Back Malaria
RDT	Rapid diagnostic test
RFA	Request for application
SANRU	*Santé Rurale*
SNAME	*Systèmed'Approvisionnement en MédicamentsEssentiels*

SNIS	*Système National d'Information Sanitaire*
SP	Sulfadoxine-pyrimethamine
UNICEF	United Nations Children's Fund
USAID	United States Agency for International Development
USG	United States Government
WHO	World Health Organization

I.   EXECUTIVE SUMMARY

The President's Malaria Initiative (PMI) is a core component of the United States Government (USG) Foreign Assistance Strategy. PMI was launched in June 2005 as a 5-year, $1.2 billion initiative to rapidly scale up malaria prevention and treatment interventions and reduce malaria-related mortality by 50% in 15 high-burden countries in sub-Saharan Africa. With the passage of the 2008 Lantos-Hyde Act, PMI was extended, and, as part of the GHI, the goal of PMI has been adjusted to reduce malaria-related mortality by 70% in the original 15 countries by the end of 2015. This will be achieved by continuing to scale up coverage of the most vulnerable groups — children under five years of age and pregnant women — with proven preventive and therapeutic interventions, including artemisinin-based combination therapies (ACTs), insecticide-treated nets (ITNs), intermittent preventive treatment of pregnant women (IPTp), and indoor residual spraying (IRS).[1]

Since PMI's inception in the Democratic Republic of Congo (DRC) in FY 2011, the United States Government (USG) funding for malaria control efforts in the DRC has significantly increased from $18 million in FY 2010 to $50 million in FY 2014. Malaria is a major health problem in the DRC, accounting for an estimated 40% of outpatient visits by children under five and 19% of the overall mortality in children under five. The implementation of large-scale malaria control activities in the DRC continues to face serious challenges. The country's health infrastructure is very weak and it is estimated that only 37% of the population has access to adequate health facilities.

The recently released preliminary report of the 2013-2014 Demographic and Health Survey (DHS) shows that the DRC is making progress with very promising malaria indicators and all-cause mortality compared to the 2010 Multiple Indicator Cluster Survey (MICS) results. A few highlights from the report include: a) the increase in the use of ITNs by children under five, from 38% to 56%; b) the increase of ITN use by pregnant women, from 43% to 60%; c) the increase of households owning at least one ITN, from 51% to70%; and d) the malaria prevalence in

---

[1]IRS is not included in the DRC PMI strategy due to cost and the great size of the country.

children under five, with a rate of 30.8% obtained by rapid diagnostic tests (RDTs), and 22.6% obtained through microscopy tests. The under-five mortality decreased from 158/1,000 live births in 2010 to 104/1,000 live births in 2013, a 30% decrease. However, these gains are tempered by reductions in malaria treatment for children. In 2013, only 29.2% of children with fevers were treated with antimalarials, whereas in 2010, 39% were treated. This reduction may have been caused by stockouts of antimalarials due to the weak supply chain throughout the country.

The support of PMI to the Ministry of Health of the DRC is based on the needs described in the National Strategic Plan 2013-2015. The main objective of this plan is to improve the health status of the population through the reduction of the human burden and economic consequences attributable to malaria. Since 2011, PMI focused on assisting the National Malaria Control Program (NMCP) health facilities within 70 targeted health zones in 4 provinces (East and West Kasai, South Kivu, and Katanga). PMI has progressively expanded its support to malaria control activities in the DRC from 70 health zones in 4 provinces to 138 health zones in 5 provinces with FY 2012 and FY 2013 resources.

In 2014, the Government of the DRC (GDRC) submitted a concept note to the Global Fund in order to obtain a total of $304.9 million for malaria prevention and control activities. With this support, the coverage of health zones by the Global Fund will increase from 219 to 308. The U.K. Department for International Development (DFID) will cover 56 health zones with its 5-year $275 million Integrated Health Project. The Korean International Agency for Development (KOICA) will support five additional health zones. As the World Bank's support to malaria is ending, some health zones will be covered by PMI and possibly other donors. With the support of all donors in malaria, the entire country will soon be covered with the minimum package of malaria services.

This FY 2015 Malaria Operational Plan (MOP) was developed during a planning field visit carried out May 19-29, 2014 with participation of staff from USAID/Kinshasa, USAID/Washington, and the Centers for Disease Control and Prevention (CDC)/Atlanta, the NMCP, and other major partners through a consultative process. The activities that PMI proposes to support are aligned with the NMCP's strategic plan. With FY 2015 funds, PMI will support 181 health zones in 6 provinces, representing almost 35% of the 516 health zones in the country. The selection of 5 health zones in the Kinshasa Province, among the new 43 health zones, is due to the large number of the population that needs access to the minimum package of malaria services in that Province.

PMI FY 2015 funding supports essential activities of USAID's Country Development Cooperation Strategy (CDCS) 2015-2019. The recently approved strategy seeks to capitalize on key opportunities to achieve the following goal: "Long-term transition to more effective and empowering development in the DRC supported." In order to achieve this, USAID will support three objectives: "1) Selected national level institutions more effectively implement their mandates; 2) Lives improved through coordinated development approaches in select regions; and, 3) Foundation for durable peace strengthened in eastern DRC." Through PMI's efforts to strengthen the capacity to implement the DRC's National Malaria Plan at the national level and at all levels of the system in select areas of the country, the FY 2015 MOP supports essential activities of the Mission's strategy for sustainable development. The proposed budget for FY 2015 is $45 million. The following paragraphs describe current progress to date as well as the FY 2015 plans:

Insecticide-treated nets (ITNs): The NMCP's National Malaria Control Strategy 2013-2015 supports free distribution of long-lasting insecticide-treated mosquito nets (LLIN) through antenatal care (ANC) and vaccination clinics; free distribution of nets through mass campaigns; and the sale of LLINs in the commercial sector. The DRC has started a nationwide, universal coverage campaign. In 2013, more than 1.2 million LLINs were distributed in PMI-supported health zones. In addition, in 2014 PMI-funded a pilot study to evaluate continuous distribution to maintain coverage between campaigns. As a result of this study, PMI plans to support the NMCP to pilot a continuous distribution program during the next two years that will be evaluated before considering scaling-up. PMI will continue to support mass distribution campaigns in 2014 with the distribution of 5.7 million nets in the provinces of Kasai Occidental and Equateur. With FY 2015 funding, PMI will procure 3 million LLINs for distribution through mass campaigns and through antenatal care and immunization services.

Indoor residual spraying (IRS): The revised NMCP Strategic Plan includes IRS, but this activity is not being implemented. Limited spraying in the country is carried out by mining companies which spray the homes of their workers in villages surrounding their compounds. Current PMI support is being used to conduct standard entomological surveillance including species identification and insecticide resistance, and to build capacity of key personnel to conduct and manage an entomological surveillance program. With FY 2015 funds, PMI will continue to support surveillance and support capacity building within the NMCP and other national structures to conduct entomological surveillance.

Prevention of malaria in pregnancy: Antenatal care is an excellent platform on which to build the malaria in pregnancy program in the DRC as more than 88% of women in the DRC attend an ANC visit at least once during their pregnancies. Although implementation of intermittent preventive treatment for pregnant women (IPTp) in the DRC began in 2006, scale-up has been slow. In 2015, PMI's support to IPTp scale-up will expand to 181 health zones in the 6 targeted provinces, where PMI plans to support procurement and distribution of sulfadoxine-pyrimethamine (SP) for IPTp; provision of refresher training of health workers, including training on treatment of malaria in pregnancy; and behavior change communication (BCC) to increase demand for and use of IPTp. The emphasis in FY 2015 will be to provide refresher training to providers on the recent changes to IPTp policy and to expand IPTp to every ANC visit after the first trimester. With FY 2015 funding, PMI will procure 3 million SP treatments to meet expected needs in PMI-targeted health zones. PMI will also procure LLINs for distribution in ANC clinics (described in the ITN section) and artemisinin-based combination therapy (ACT) and quinine (described under case management) for use in the treatment of malaria in pregnant women.

Malaria case management and pharmaceutical system management: In previous years, PMI has supported the supply chain management system in the DRC and antimalarial treatment policies. These activities include the scale-up of antimalarial treatment with artesunate-amodiaquine (AS-AQ), the implementation of a pilot evaluation for the use of rectal artesunate for pre-referral of severe cases and training of healthcare workers in malaria diagnostics using microscopy and rapid diagnostic tests (RDTs). PMI has also been involved in improving case management at the community level via the integrated community case management (iCCM) platform. These efforts have led to considerable improvements in timely access to antimalarial treatment.

With FY 2015 funding, PMI support will expand to 181 health zones in 6 provinces, with procurement of 10 million RDTs, 7.5 million AS-AQ treatments, and 340,000 treatments for severe malaria. PMI will also support training and supervision of health workers in case management. In addition, PMI will provide technical assistance to the NMCP and Ministry of Health (MOH) to strengthen the supply chain and pharmaceutical management systems at the national, provincial, and health zone levels in those six provinces, working directly with NMCP staff to quantify drug needs and assist in the implementation of more efficient stock and distribution systems. PMI funds will be used to procure 600,000 doses of rectal artesunate for pre-referral treatment for cases of severe malaria identified at the community level. Finally, PMI will support the scale-up of iCCM sites with RDTs and ACTs for uncomplicated cases and rectal artesunate for pre-referral treatments of severe cases.

Monitoring and evaluation (M&E): The PMI strategy to support M&E focuses on three levels: national, provincial, and health zone. At the national level, PMI supports improved data analysis and use through training and provision of an M&E technical advisor to the NMCP. At the provincial level, PMI will support regional technical advisors who play an important role in the synthesis and analysis of data at the provincial NMCP offices, as well as supervise M&E activities within the health zones. PMI will also provide limited funds for malaria outbreak investigations at the provincial level. At the health zone level, PMI will work with its bilateral partners and the national health information system to strengthen data collection and management and provide enhanced monitoring of epidemiological and entomological data at selected health zones in selected focal provinces. In terms of national level data collection, PMI will support the end-use verification survey, the net durability assessment, and the 2015-2016 Malaria Indicator Survey (MIS). Following the MIS, PMI will provide technical and financial support to conduct an impact evaluation to show progress made towards reducing child mortality. This impact evaluation will further analyze several data sources (DHS, MIS, program data) to demonstrate the impact of all PMI investments in the country.

Operational research: The PMI/ DRC team proposes to support an operational research project focused on monitoring insecticide resistance in *Anopheles gambiae*, the primary malaria vector present in Kinshasa, over the course of a year during which a mass LLIN distribution campaign is planned. Resistance will be monitored using CDC bottle bioassays, including the intensity bioassay, and resistance mechanisms will be determined using standard molecular methods. The results will be used to inform the entomological profile of the DRC and to guide decisions regarding vector control.

Behavior change communication (BCC): Since its inception in the DRC, PMI has supported BCC activities in targeted health zones to promote use of malaria preventive measures and treatment services. The malaria package of services has been supported with an array of BCC activities ranging from mass media to support the LLIN mass distribution campaigns, community radio spots, short message service, community mobilization, training of healthcare providers, and interpersonal communication. These efforts have aimed to increase the use of ACTs as a first-line treatment for malaria, increase coverage of IPTp for prevention of malaria in pregnancy, increase the use of LLINs, sensitize communities on malaria symptoms and danger signs, and promote treatment-seeking behavior.

In FY 2015, PMI will continue to support implementation of the national communication strategy in PMI-supported health zones. BCC activities will be focused on raising awareness of health workers, religious leaders, community health workers, community groups, school students and other malaria stakeholders on the importance of malaria prevention and treatment. BCC messages will be integrated into BCC activities throughout the health portfolio to leverage the effectiveness and reach of interventions. PMI will also engage government officials, donors, parliamentarians and the private sector for greater advocacy for increased resources for malaria control, and for greater coordination of BCC activities in the health sector.

Health system strengthening and capacity building: PMI continues to support the health system to deliver the minimum package of malaria services in health facilities, and promote the use of preventive measures and case management services at the community level. The supply chain management and distribution system continues to pose serious challenges to the delivery of services, creating recurrent stockouts of malaria commodities, mainly ACTs and SP, due to the lack of quality consumption data to quantify commodity needs. Also, despite efforts to improve the leadership of the NMCP and reinvigorate the program staff, the capacity to coordinate still needs improvement. During the past 12 months, PMI has increased its support to strengthen the health system by adding an additional in-country supply chain management partner to facilitate the procurement of commodities and improve distribution of commodities to end users. PMI has also invested in capacity building to improve the logistics management information system (LMIS) and the health management information system (HMIS), and increased access to malaria technical knowledge and practices by health officers and service providers. In FY 2015, PMI will continue to support enhanced capacity building, particularly the implementation of the recommendations from the assessment of NMCP organizational capabilities, training service providers and supportive supervision in new health zones, as well as increasing storage and management capacity of the supply chain.

II. STRATEGY

A. Introduction

The President's Malaria Initiative (PMI) is a core component of the Global Health Initiative (GHI), along with HIV/AIDS, and tuberculosis. PMI was launched in June 2005 as a 5-year, $1.2 billion initiative to rapidly scale up malaria prevention and treatment interventions and reduce malaria-related mortality by 50% in 15 high-burden countries in sub-Saharan Africa. With passage of the 2008 Lantos-Hyde Act, funding for PMI has now been extended and, as part of the GHI, the goal of PMI has been adjusted to reduce malaria-related mortality by 70% in the original 15 countries by the end of 2015. This will be achieved by continuing to scale up coverage of the most vulnerable groups — children under five years of age and pregnant women — with proven preventive and therapeutic interventions, including artemisinin-based combination therapies (ACTs), insecticide-treated nets (ITNs), intermittent preventive treatment of pregnant women (IPTp), and indoor residual spraying (IRS).

The Democratic Republic of the Congo (DRC) was selected as a PMI country in FY 2011. Over the last five years, the DRC has received substantial USAID support for malaria activities: FY 2009, $15 million; FY 2010, $18 million; FY 2011, $34.9 million; FY 2012, $38 million; FY 2013, $41.9 million, and in FY 2014, $50 million.

This FY 2015 Malaria Operational Plan (MOP) presents a detailed implementation plan for the DRC based on PMI's multi-year strategy and the National Malaria Control Program (NMCP)'s revised three-year strategy. It was developed in consultation with the NMCP, and with participation of national and international partners involved with malaria prevention and control in the country. The activities that PMI is proposing are aligned with the National Malaria Control Strategy and Plan and will build on investments made by PMI and other partners to improve and expand malaria-related services, including the Global Fund to Fight AIDS, Tuberculosis, and Malaria (Global Fund) malaria grants. In 2014, the Government of the DRC submitted a concept note to the Global Fund in order to obtain a total of $304.9 million for malaria prevention and control activities. With this support, the coverage of health zones will be increased from 219 to 308. The U.K. Department for International Development (DFID) will cover 56 health zones with the awarded 5-year $275 million Integrated Health Project. The Korean International Agency for Development (KOICA) will support five additional health zones. As the World Bank's support to Malaria is ending, some health zones will be taken by PMI or other donors.

This section briefly describes the country malaria situation, the current status of malaria control strategy in the DRC, the coordination mechanisms with other partners and funders, and the progress on coverage and impact indicators. Finally, this section summarizes the challenges, opportunities, and threats for malaria prevention and control in the DRC and provides a description of PMI's support strategy for FY 2015.

This MOP was developed during a planning field visit carried out on May -29, 2014 with participation of USAID/Kinshasa, USAID/Washington, and the Centers for Disease Control and Prevention (CDC)/Atlanta, the NMCP, and other major partners, through a consultative process. The activities that PMI proposes to support are aligned with the NMCP's strategic plan. With FY

2015 funds, PMI will support 181 health zones in 6 provinces, representing almost 35% of the 516 health zones in the country.

Furthermore, PMI FY 2015 funding will support essential activities of USAID's Country Development Cooperation Strategy (CDCS) 2013-2018. The recently approved strategy seeks to capitalize on key opportunities to achieve the following goal: long-term transition to more effective and empowering development in the DRC supported. In order to achieve this, USAID will support three objectives: 1) selected national level institutions more effectively implement their mandates; 2) lives improved through coordinated development approaches in select regions; and 3) foundation for durable peace strengthened in eastern the DRC. Through PMI's efforts to strengthen the capacity to implement the DRC's National Malaria Plan at the national level and at all levels of the system in select areas of the country, the FY 2015 MOP supports essential activities of the USAID Mission's strategy for sustainable development. The proposed budget for FY 2015 is $45 million, which will be spent on activities summarized later in this plan.

B. Malaria Situation in the DRC

The Democratic Republic of the Congo is the second largest country in Africa (after Algeria) and the third most populated in Africa. It has a population that is estimated to be 75.5 million people, the majority of whom live in rural areas. It shares borders with nine countries—Congo Brazzaville, Central African Republic, Sudan, Uganda, Rwanda, Burundi, Tanzania, Zambia, and Angola—the last six of which are PMI focus countries. Administratively, the country is divided into 11 provinces and 45 districts, although the country is in the process of further subdividing into 26 provinces. The DRC is one of the poorest countries in the world, ranking at the bottom (186th out of 186 countries) in the world in terms of the 2013 human development index; an estimated 80% of the population lives on less that $1 per day. According to the Demographics and Health Survey(DHS) 2013-2014 preliminary results, the under-five mortality rate are 104/1,000 live births, a significant reduction from the previous rate of 158/1,000 (Multiple Indicator Cluster Survey 2010).

Malaria is reported by the Ministry of Health (MOH) to be the principal cause of morbidity and mortality in the DRC. It is estimated that 97% of the population lives in zones with stable transmission lasting 8 to 12 months per year (at between 300 and 1,000 meters altitude). The highest levels of transmission occur in zones situated in in the north and west of the country. The remaining 3% of the population lives in highland or mountainous areas (mostly in North Kivu, South Kivu, and Katanga Provinces), which are prone to malaria epidemics. As is the case throughout tropical Africa, the greatest burden of malaria morbidity and mortality falls on pregnant women and children under five years of age. According to MOH reports, malaria accounts for more than 40% of all outpatient visits and for 40% of deaths among children under-five years of age. In fact, because of the large population living in high transmission zones, it has been estimated that the DRC accounts for 11% of all cases of *Plasmodium falciparum* in sub-Saharan Africa.

Plasmodium falciparum, the predominant species of malaria parasite in DRC, accounts for approximately 95% of all infections. Studies carried out in 2000-2001 showed 29-80% resistance to chloroquine and up to 60% resistance with sulfadoxine-pyrimethamine (SP). In 2005, the combinations of amodiaquine plus artesunate (AS-AQ) and artesunate-lumefantrine (AL) were shown to be highly efficacious at five sites around the country, and AS-AQ was adopted as the first-line drug for the treatment of uncomplicated malaria. Data on parasitemia and anemia in DRC are patchy and mostly derived from smaller studies that do not allow for national estimates. However, the 2007 DHS collected samples from a nationally representative sample of adult women and showed that 34% were parasitemic in PCR testing. The same survey showed that 71% of Congolese children aged 6-59 months were anemic, which is closely associated with malaria infection.

The primary vector of malaria in DRC is *Anopheles gambiaes.s.* There are several secondary vectors present in different parts of the country including *An. funestus, An. paludis,* and *An. nili.* Resistance to dichlorodiphenyltrichloroethane (DDT) and pyrethroids is widespread, but little resistance to organophosphates and carbamates has been detected.

C. Country Health System and Ministry of Health

The health system in the DRC has three levels: a central level, which includes the office of the Minister of Health, the Secretary General of MOH, and the Directorates of national disease-specific programs (HIV/AIDS; TB; malaria, etc.); an intermediate level composed of 11 provincial health departments and 48 administrative health districts; and the peripheral level with 516 health zones with more than 6,000 health centers (approximately 15-20 health centers per health zone). Over half of all health zones are supported by faith-based organizations (FBOs) or other non-governmental organizations (NGOs). The health system also uses two types of unpaid community-based workers called community "*relais*." Community health promoters (promotion *relais*) carry out health promotion and community mobilization activities, while community treatment workers (treatment *relais*) deliver a limited set of interventions (i.e. treatment of diarrhea, fever, and referral of malnourished children to health facilities, plus distribution of a limited range of family planning commodities). Community treatment workers are selected based on a higher level of education and having an established source of remuneration, independent of their health work.

Each of the 516 health zones has a general referral hospital. Faith-based organizations run 34% of these hospitals, which are integrated into the public health system. In most health zones supported by FBOs and NGOs, MOH pays government workers' salaries, which are extremely low ($25 per month), and provides additional salary supplemental incentives, known as *primes*. FBOs and NGOs often provide additional *primes* to health workers as well as providing essential drugs, laboratory equipment, commodities, and in-service training. As of 2009, MOH estimates that 256 health zones—roughly half—are supported through service delivery contracts with FBOs or NGOs.

The DRC has a tiered essential medicines supply system under the National Essential Medicine Supply Program, consisting of a centralized pharmaceutical procurement system through the nonprofit association (Federation of Essential Medicine Procurement Agencies), combined with a decentralized warehousing and distribution system supported by existing distribution hubs. The USG, European Union, and Belgium Corporation are providing significant technical assistance

3

in supply chain management at various levels of the system to build country pharmaceutical management and drugs distribution capacity.

The national government has made the decision to subdivide the existing 11 provinces into 26 new ones, and this process is expected to start during this year of 2014. MOH has issued a decree establishing new provincial health departments within each of the 26 new provinces. The MOH is also in the process of restructuring. In the current plans, the NMCP will become a unit of the Disease Control Directorate by 2015.

Figure 1: Administrative map of the Democratic Republic of the Congo

D. National Malaria Control Strategy

The malaria control program of the DRC is based on a National Malaria Strategic Plan, which was first developed in 2002 following the Abuja Summit and has been revised several times to keep pace with recommendations from the World Health Organization and Roll Back Malaria. The former Strategic Plan (2009-2013) called for scaling up of key interventions with a goal of reducing malaria burden (morbidity and mortality) by 75% by 2015, compared with a 2000 baseline. The current National Strategic Plan (2013-2015) aims at reducing malaria mortality by 50% within health facilities at the end of 2015, compared to the mortality reported in 2010.

4

The focus of the NMCP is: a) the strengthening of prevention activities through methods of individual and collective protection, such as ITNs, IRS, the treatment of mosquito breeding sites, and the improvement of housing and environment; b) prevention of malaria during pregnancy through IPTp; c) improvement of early case management, with appropriate treatment at all levels of the health system; and d) reinforcement of management of epidemics due to malaria.

In early 2013, a Malaria Program Review (MPR) was conducted in the DRC that assessed the performance of the NMCP and resulted in a number of recommendations for strengthening the malaria control program. The report called for improvements in the scaling up of diagnostics, and strengthening of the supply chain and pharmaceutical system, as well as improvements in general program management. These recommendations have been taken into account in the current 2013-2015 National Strategic Plan. The targets of the plan are: 1) Malaria prevention (increase bed net use to 80% among people at risk); 2) Iincrease IPTp uptake to 80% among pregnant women; 3) Appropriate case management (80% confirmed cases); 4) Appropriate response to epidemics and emergency situations (control at least 80% of outbreaks); 5) Improved program management (disburse 100% of funding allocated to the program); 6) Advocacy, IEC, and community mobilization (increase knowledge of malaria to 80%); 7) Appropriate management of commodities; and 8) Monitoring and evaluation, epidemiological surveillance, and operational research (obtain data completeness in 95% of health zones, and carry out 80% of operations research studies planned) .

E. Integration, Collaboration and Coordination

Many donors are contributing to malaria control efforts in the DRC, the most important of which are:

The Global Fund: The major donor for malaria control activities in the DRC is the Global Fund. In 2012 the Global Fund approved a Round 8-Round 10 consolidation grant with $212 million for malaria prevention and control activities in the DRC for five years (2012-2016) to accelerate malaria prevention and control in a total of 219 health zones. More recently, the Global Fund awarded $85 million transitional funding grant for 2013 and 2014 of which $55 million will be spent on procuring ITNs for distribution through mass campaign to sustain universal coverage. Recently, the NMCP submitted a concept note to the Global Fund for a total budget of a total of $ 304.9 million dollars for malaria prevention and control activities. With this support, the coverage of health zones will be increased from 219 to 308.

The World Bank: The Booster Program has been supporting malaria control in the DRC since 2006 through two World Bank projects: 1) the DRC Health Sector Rehabilitation Project, a 4-year, $150 million project, of which $36 million supports malaria prevention and treatment services in 83 health zones, that ends in June 2014; and 2) a $180 million Emergency Urban and Social Rehabilitation Project that included a $13 million, one-time procurement and distribution of 2 million ITNs. The last additional specific allotment for malaria was a $100 million project called Booster Program Phase II which supported universal coverage of bed nets and malaria interventions in 63 health zones and ended in June 2013. In early May 2014, the World Bank announced the development of a new grant for the DRC for a total of $1 billion for all sectors, but the size of the malaria component in the new grant is as yet unknown.

The Department for International Development: The Department for International Development (DFID) recently awarded a 5-year £182 million (~$275 million) integrated health project in 56 health zones with a malaria component. Some of these health zones overlap with the PMI expansion project areas. Additionally, £39.5 million (~$60 million) will support ongoing ITN distribution campaigns in two to three provinces, as well as strengthen NMCP capacity and support the introduction of ACTs in the private sector.

PMI: In FY 2015, PMI will expand its support and will cover 181 health zones in 6 provinces, representing almost 35% of the 516 health zones in the country, and continue to focus on targeted technical assistance to the NMCP and field implementation of activities.

In addition to the above-mentioned major donors, support for malaria control will continue to come from UNICEF, KOICA in five health zones, the Sweden International Development Agency, the Canadian International Development Agency, and WHO. Since 2006, the Government of the DRC has provided approximately $2 million annually to the NMCP for staffing costs, infrastructure, and some commodities. Funding for salary support has continued at about the same level but no funding is provided for commodities. The Government of the DRC (GDRC) has recently contributed $500,000 in cost share to the Global Fund. Support from the private sector has come from by the TenkeFungurume Mining Company, which has conducted yearly rounds of IRS since 2008 as a part of their malaria control program in 10 of 18 health areas in the Fungurume Health Zone, in Katanga Province. This program, which included universal coverage with ITNs, achieved a 60% reduction in incidence of malaria in the workforce and a 56% reduction of malaria prevalence in school age children. Although donors plan to conduct policy dialogue with the government on health sector financing, there is no information currently available on whether the GODRC plans to increase the proportion of its national budget allocated to the health sector.

The DRC has five communication and coordination mechanisms for the health sector:

- The **Steering Committee for the Coordination of National Health Development Plan** (*Comité National de Pilotage*) is the highest level coordination mechanism established by MOH to oversee the implementation of the next five-year National Health Development Plan (PNDS 2011-2015).
- The **Donors Group** (also called *Group Inter Bailleurs Santé*) meets monthly to plan and coordinate activities throughout the country, such as the ITN mass distribution campaigns.
- The **Country Coordinating Mechanism (CCM)**, which meets regularly with health sector stakeholders to review options and plans for submission of proposals to the Global Fund, to keep abreast of progress towards start-up of activities and grant implementation, and to provide administrative and financial oversight of the principal recipients. The CCM does not have any direct role in implementation of malaria activities. The PMI staff and the USAID Global Fund liaison have participated in developing and reviewing country proposal submissions. USAID co-chairs the CCM as the first vice-president, and also provides technical assistance through the Global Fund Liaison Advisor and through the USAID-funded Grant.

- The **Malaria Technical Working Group – Task Force**: This open forum is chaired by the Disease Control Directorate and meets quarterly for coordination and technical discussions at the national level as well as with each province. Meetings also include representatives of civil society and, more recently, the private sector. During the development of the PMI FY 2015 MOP, the Task Force meeting was held and the MOP team members participated. The group has improved donor coordination, as illustrated by improved joint planning for certain provinces to revise the map of malaria donor assistance in the country.
- The **PMI Partners' Meeting**: Initiated in April 2011, NMCP, PMI and partners meet quarterly for program review and coordination.

Figure 2: The Democratic Republic of the Congo Malaria Donors' distribution map

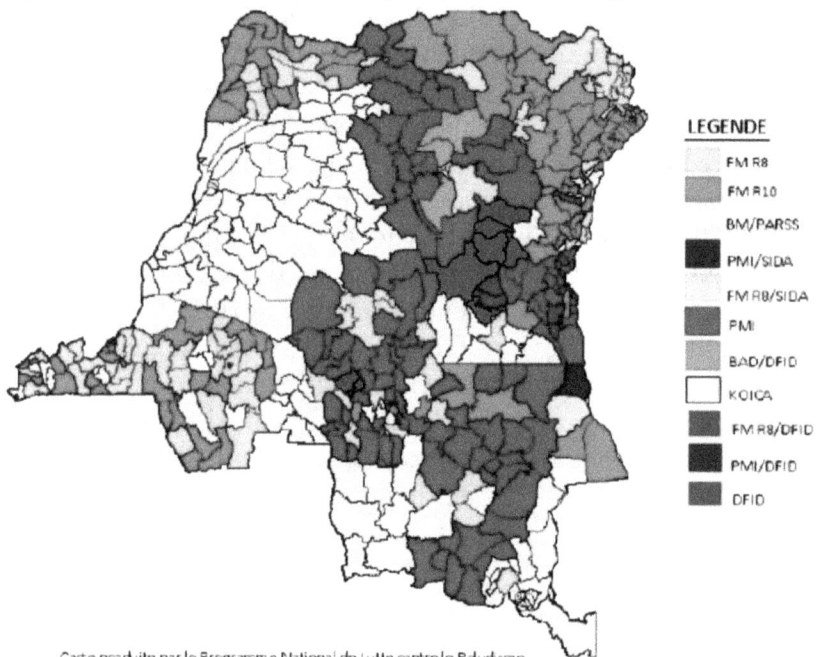

Carte produite par le Programme National de Lutte contre le Paludisme

F. PMI Goals and Objectives

In the DRC, PMI aims to expand malaria control efforts through reaching large areas with key interventions, achieving a 50% reduction in malaria burden (morbidity and mortality) in at-risk populations when compared with the 2007 baseline established in the DRC's Demographic and Health Survey (DHS). By the end of 2015, PMI will assist the DRC to achieve the following targets in populations at risk for malaria:

- More than 90% of households with a pregnant woman and/or children under five will own at least one ITN;
- 85% of children under five will have slept under an ITN the previous night;
- 85% of pregnant women will have slept under an ITN the previous night;
- 85% of pregnant women and children under five will have slept under an ITN the previous night or in a house that has been sprayed with IRS in the last 6 months when appropriate;

- 85% of women who have completed a pregnancy in the last two years will have received two or more doses of IPTp during that pregnancy;
- 85% of government health facilities will have ACTs available for treatment of uncomplicated malaria; and
- 85% of children under five with suspected malaria will have received treatment with an ACT within 24 hours of onset of their symptoms.

G. Progress on Indicators to Date

The most up-to-date information on the status of malaria prevention and control interventions in the DRC comes from the 2013 DHS. NMCP targets for 2015 are also summarized in Table 1 below.

The recently released preliminary report of the 2013-2014 DHS, shows that the DRC is making progress with very promising malaria indicators and all-cause mortality compared to the 2010 Multiple Indicator Cluster Survey (MICS) results. A few highlights from the report include: a) the increase in the use of ITNs by children under five, from 38% to 56%; b) the increase of ITN use by the pregnant women, from 43% to 60%; c) the increase of households owning at least one ITN, from 51% to70%; and d) the malaria prevalence in children under five, with a rate of 30.8% obtained by RTDs, and 22.6% obtained through microscopy tests. The under-five mortality decreased from 158/1,000 live births in 2010 to 104/1,000 live births in 2013. However, these gains are tempered by reductions in malaria treatment for children. In 2013, only 29.2% of children with fevers were treated with antimalarials, whereas in 2010, 39% were treated.

Table 1: Results of 2007 DHS, 2010 MICS, and 2013 DHS

Indicator	2007 DHS	MICS 2010	2013 DHS	NMCP 2015 Targets
Households with ≥ 1 ITN	9%	51%	70%	>80%
Children ≤ 5 sleeping under an ITN the previous night	6%	38%	55.9%	>80%
Pregnant women who slept under an ITN the previous night	7%	43%	60.3%	>80%
Women who received ≥ 2 doses of IPTp during their last pregnancy in the last two years	5%	N/A	14.3%	>80%
Children ≤ 5 with fever in the last two weeks who received antimalarial treatment	39.9%	N/A	29.9%	85%
Children ≤ 5 with fever in the last two weeks who received treatment with an ACT within 24 hours of onset of fever	<1%*	N/A	1.8%	>80%
Malaria Prevalence	N/A	N/A	30.85% RDTs 22.6% Microscopy	N/A

*Although a total of 17% of children under five received an antimalarial drug the same day or next day after onset of fever, most were treated with quinine; SP and amodiaquine were also prescribed.

Table 2: Major data collection for malaria program monitoring in the DRC 2007-2015

Data Source	2007	2008-2009	2010	2011	2012	2013	2014	2015
Household Surveys	DHS 2007 (Report available)		MICS 2010 (Report available)			DHS 2013 (final report in progress)	National Census?	MIS 2015
Other surveys					EUV 2012 (Report Available)	EUV 2013 (Report available)	EUV 2014 (Report available)	EUV 2015
Surveillance and Routine Support					Ongoing	Ongoing	Ongoing	Ongoing
Other data sources				Partner reports	Partner reports	Partner reports	Partner reports	Partner reports

G. Other Relevant Evidence on Progress

No other major surveillance has been conducted during this year of 2014, except for the DHS carried out in 2013.

H. Challenges, Opportunities, and Threats

Challenges in the DRC continue to be the same in controlling malaria and effectively monitoring all malaria activities in the country. These include: 1) an inefficient supply chain management system due to poor infrastructure and a lack of adequate and sufficient resources; 2) a deficient Health Management Information System (HMIS), where the quality of the information is still low, and the data are incomplete and inaccurate; 3) lack of sufficient personnel at the central and provincial levels to manage the system and the ever-expanding activities necessary to fight malaria; 4) deficient monitoring and evaluation systems due to the lack of human and logistic resources; 5) vast geographical scope of the program where geography plays an important role in access and coverage of interventions; 6) inaccessible areas due to conflict or civil unrest; 7) lack of adequate communication systems; and 8) low quality of malaria diagnostics due to lack of qualified personnel and stock outs of diagnostic commodities.

Supply Chain Management

One of the greatest threats to all malaria activities in the country is the weak supply chain and logistics system for drugs and all malaria commodities. Providing effective antimalarial treatment in the DRC is one of the biggest challenges for PMI. The weak pharmaceutical system in a country as vast as the DRC poses a major challenge. PMI can be quite effective in delivering antimalarial drugs and diagnostic supplies to regional distribution warehouses, since this phase of the distribution system is done independently from the country supply chain system and is now facilitated by the in-country presence of one of its implementers. However, distribution of

PMI commodities for routine use from warehouses down to health zones and health facilities is done through the DRC's country supply chain system. Health zone and health facility staff face numerous challenges to properly estimate needs and in finding transportation to pick up drugs at warehouses.

Health Management Information Systems

Quality data emanating from health facilities should be fed to the provincial and then central levels, but at present the data is far from accurate and reliable. Much still needs to be done to improve the system. The Ministry of Health has started with the implementation of the new HMIS system, which is right now in its first phase of implementation. It is expected to take a couple of years to have it running throughout the whole country. In the meantime, parallel information systems run simultaneously, making the collection of data difficult to obtain and even analyze.

Human Resources

The healthcare sector in the DRC is plagued by rapid turn-over of employees, who move on to new positions for both financial and political reasons. At the same time, the MOH does not have any system for recording training activities and which employees benefited from various courses. This creates a number of challenges to provide refresher training as new policies are rolled out. Many clinicians still provide services based on how they were trained in nursing or medical school, which does not always correspond to the most recent recommendations. Attention needs to be devoted to improving utilization rates of public health system in the DRC and healthcare workers compliance with treatment regimens. The low uptake of ACTs in the DRC can be attributed to poor utilization of the public health system, poor acceptability of AS-AQ by both health workers and patients, and finally the financial incentive to use other antimalarial drugs available for purchase. A health facility evaluation is planned for late 2014 to provide comprehensive information on the issues around the provision of care. Additionally, low salaries lead employees to seek means to obtain additional funds and, in many cases, to perform at low quality standards.

Monitoring and Evaluation (M&E)

Even though, the NMCP has issued its plan for monitoring and evaluation, the low number of human as well as logistic resources at the NMCP for managerial and supervisory functions constitutes a significant threat to the long-term efficiency and sustainability of high-impact malaria activities. PMI has hired an advisor to support the NMCP at the central M&E unit to address this concern, and has developed plans to work with the *Système National d'Information Sanitaire* (SNIS) (National Health Information Management System) to pilot improvements in the M&E system. In many cases, it is very difficult to access health facilities for proper monitoring and evaluation visits. However, lack of M&E visits exists at all levels, from the central to the provincial level; from the provincial level to the health zone; and from the health zone to the health facilities.

Access to Health Services and Coverage

Another critical gap is coverage of remote health zones in the hard-to-reach regions of the country due to geographical characteristics of the regions. There is an overall lack of roads and physical infrastructure which renders many health zones inaccessible. Continually stocking of commodities and performing supervision in these zones continues to be a great challenge, and greatly increases the cost of doing business. Additionally, a large portion of the population does not have access to health facilities in remote regions. In 2013, PMI expanded into Oriental Province, and in 2015 PMI will absorb, depending on different factors, an additional 43 health zones, thus bringing the minimum package of malaria services to these remote areas.

Conflict and Civil Unrest
The instability in Eastern Congo is a major threat to the implementation and monitoring of projects. Ongoing projects have not been able to properly monitor activities in this region because they cannot access project sites due to the security situation. Activities have been halted and scaled back, since many health workers have been afraid to work, or have had to flee some areas.

Communication Challenges
The major challenges to effectively implement a BCC plan in the DRC are the size of the country, the lack of infrastructure to disseminate BCC materials and messages, and the wide range of languages spoken by the population. In a country with four national languages and over 200 dialects, vernacular is a key to successful communication. Materials developed should be in the local language of the target audience, as well as be able to address the high levels of illiteracy among target populations. Furthermore, the lack of infrastructure, both physical and technological, greatly complicates the dissemination of BCC products and messages. But these challenges are tempered by the existence of a variety of communication channels, including traditional channels, radio, and television that can be used to air messages to target populations.

Diagnostics
The DRC faces several challenges related to malaria diagnosis and RDT testing. First, despite the recent progress to rehabilitate and provide refreshment training to microscopists in the DRC, it is likely that the functional laboratory capacity will continue to be low across the country. Second, although the national policy calls for confirmation of all malaria cases, there are frequent stockouts of RDTs and a lack of trained health facility and community workers to perform these tests. In many cases, laboratory test results are not taken into account before administering antimalarial treatment. Finally, a number of private laboratories with variable expertise exist in the DRC and little is known about the accuracy of malaria diagnosis in these facilities.

Despite the huge challenges, the DRC also benefits from strong support of many donors. Funding has been increasing from other donors such as the Global Fund and DFID, and other international partners planning a minimum package of malaria interventions in each of the 516 health zones of the country. Appropriate collaboration and coordination among donors is required to ensure efficient and sustainable technical assistance and implementation support to the NMCP.

I. PMI Support Strategy

The support of PMI to the MOH of the DRC is based on the needs described in the National Strategic Plan 2013-2015, where the main objective is to contribute to the improvement of the health status of the population through the reduction of the human burden and economic consequences attributable to malaria. Since 2011, PMI focused to assist the National Malaria Control Program (NMCP) health facilities within 70 targeted health zones in 4 provinces (East and West Kasai, South Kivu, and Katanga). With FY 2012 and FY 2013 resources, PMI has progressively expanded its support to 138 health zones in 5 provinces.

III. OPERATIONAL PLAN

A. Insecticide-treated nets

NMCP/PMI Objectives
The revised NMCP Strategic Plan continues to focus on achieving high long-lasting insecticide-treated net (LLIN) availability and use among the general population by ensuring that at least 80% of persons at risk of malaria sleep under an LLIN. The NMCP follows a three-pronged strategy for distributing LLINs: distribution of free LLIN through large-scale integrated or stand-alone campaigns; routine distribution of free nets to pregnant women during antenatal care (ANC) and to children less than five years of age at pre-school vaccination clinics (final measles vaccination); and private sector sales of full-cost nets.

The strategy for achieving universal coverage (defined as one LLIN per 1.8 persons, as per WHO guidelines) is to distribute nets via a voucher system as follows: 1) one net to a household of one to two persons, two nets to a family of three to five persons, three to that of six to eight, and four to a household of greater than nine; and 2) one net per bed or sleeping space through mass campaigns for hospitals and boarding schools. In the absence of information on LLIN durability, the NMCP recommends replacing nets every three years. The NMCP completed its first cycle of universal coverage at the end of 2013 and is now beginning replacement campaigns.

Progress since PMI was launched
In 2011 and early 2012, the DRC and international partners (DFID, GF, PMI, PSI, UNICEF, World Bank) distributed more than 20 million LLINs in universal coverage campaigns in seven provinces. To assist the DRC in scaling up universal coverage, PMI procured and paid for distribution costs of 2 million LLINs of the 5.3 million needed to support a mass net distribution in Katanga, the country's most populous province. The World Bank and UNICEF supported procurement and distribution of the remaining 3.3 million. Although nets were procured in 2011, LLIN distribution was delayed until April 2012, due to the general elections in November 2011.

Coordinating donor contributions is a key component of the ITN program and a major responsibility of the NMCP. In FY 2010 and FY 2011, USAID provided funding to support the development of a centralized database for LLINs to improve the NMCP's ability to track inputs geographically and target its funding requests. The development of this database is ongoing and the functionality will be assessed during the organizational assessment of the NMCP (discussed elsewhere in the MOP). PMI Resident Advisors continue to work closely with the NMCP to help build its coordination capacity and help monitor the implementation of this centralized database. With PMI support, NMCP and partners have developed a national integrated BCC strategy for malaria control interventions, which includes the promotion of correct ITN use. PMI supported

BCC activities during the Global Fund Round 8 mass ITN distribution in 3 of the 11 provinces in 2011, and in one province in 2012.

To sustain ITN coverage post-campaign, the National Strategy includes distribution of ITNs through routine ANC and pre-school clinics, but the distribution network and infrastructure are inadequate to ensure sufficient and regular supplies. Monitoring the routine distribution of nets is a challenge and the costs of transporting nets from ports to distribution points have been higher than originally anticipated, due to the poor road network. Nets are transported using boats or airplanes when they are delivered to Matadi Port in Kinshasa or in the provinces, and trucks are generally used to transport them from neighboring countries. Nevertheless, the NMCP and partners stress the importance of continuing some level of support for the routine system. Approximately 867,745 ITNs were distributed through ANCs and child clinics nationwide up to and including 2012.

Although difficulties in logistics and transportation have hindered the routine system, in 2011 314,000 ITNs were distributed in ANCs and child care clinics in 70 of the 138 health zones. During 2012, PMI distributed only 114,000 of a projected 455,000 ITNs in the same 70 health zones because of the NMCP policy to halt routine ITN distribution before and during a mass campaign. Thus, health zones in South Kivu and Katanga were not "eligible" for routine distribution for the latter part of 2012 and early 2013. Also, shipments of PMI-procured LLINs have encountered some delays in FY 2013.

Progress during the past 12 months
During 2013, PMI contributed 1.2 million nets in collaboration with UNICEF for the universal coverage campaign for the Maniema Province with distribution starting in October 2013. By early 2013, some of these health zones had just begun to restart routine distribution of nets, with approximately 85,000 nets distributed in the first half of the year. Activities for routine distribution have just begun in a few of the 68 recently covered health zones. To explore additional strategies to increase net ownership and usage, and given the perceived high cost of routine distribution, PMI supported the NMCP conduct an external review of the system for routine distribution, and preliminary results were released in May 2014.

Preliminary results from the 2013-2014 Demographic Health Survey indicate that 70% of households report owning at least ITN, a huge increase from 9% in 2007. In addition, 56% of children under five and 60% of pregnant women slept under an ITN the night before the survey, dramatic increases from 6% and 7% in 2007, respectively.

Commodity gap analysis
With the assumption of net replacement every three years, Table 3 presents the ITN distribution schedule to implement the universal coverage strategy in 2014-2016.

Table 3a: ITN Gap analysis for mass campaigns, 2014-2016

Year	Province	Estimated population to cover	Required LLINs	Gap	Funding/ partners
2014	Bas Congo	3,588,819	1,993,788	0	Global Fund/DFID
2014	Orientale	10,760,175	5,977,875	0	Global Fund
2014	Bandundu	1,939,310	1,077,394	0	Global Fund/DFID
2014	Kasai Occidental	8,500,276	4,722,376	0	USAID/PMI
2014	Kasai Oriental	9,804,641	5,447,023	0	Global Fund/DFID
2014	Equateur	1,770,218	983,454	0	USAID/PMI
	Total 2014	**36,363,439**	**20,201,910**	**0**	
2015	Nord Kivu	8,597,144	4,776,191	4,776,191	TBD
2015	Sud Kivu	10,982,047	6,101,137	6,101,137	TBD
2015	Katanga	3,807,378	2,115,210	2,115,210	TBD
2015	Bandundu	5,346,936	2,970,520	2,970,520	TBD
2015	Equateur	6,345,109	3,525,061	3,525,061	TBD
2015	Orientale	11,082,980	6,157,211	0	Global Fund
2015	Maniema	2,384,903	1,324,946	0	USAID/PMI
	Total 2015	**48,546,498**	**26,970,277**	**19,488,119**	
2016	Kinshasa	8,597,144	4,776,191	4,776,191	TBD
	Total 2016	**8,597,144**	**4,776,191**	**4,776,191**	

Table 3b: ITN Gap analysis for Routine Distribution in ANC and Child Clinics, 2014-2016

Year	2014	2015	2016
Total Population	89,023,698	91,694,409	94,445,242
Pregnant Women (4% of Population) - ANC	3,560,948	3,667,776	3,777,810
Number of children less than one year (3.49%) - EPI	3,106,927	3,200,135	3,296,139
Total need for Routine	**6,667,875**	**6,867,911**	**7,073,949**
Total Population in PMI target area	22,127,894	31,698,005	32,680,643
Pregnant Women (4% of Population)	885,116	1,267,920	1,307,226
Number of children less than one year (3.49%)	772,264	1,106,260	1,140,554
Total need for Routine in PMI target area	**1,657,379**	**2,374,181**	**2,447,780**
Nets provided by PMI*	1,600,000	1,500,000	1,500,000
GAP in PMI supported areas	57,379	874,181	947,780
Population outside PMI areas	66,895,804	59,996,404	61,764,599
Pregnant Women (4% of Population)	2,675,832	2,399,856	2,470,584
Number of children less than one year (3.49%)	2,334,664	2,093,874	2,155,585
Total need for Routine outside PMI areas	**5,010,496**	**4,493,731**	**4,626,168**
Global Fund	Nd	Nd	Nd
World Bank/UNICEF	Nd	Nd	Nd
KOICA	Nd	Nd	Nd
GAP outside PMI area (surplus)	Nd	Nd	Nd

*PMI LLINs for 2014 procured with FY 2013 funds, for 2015 with FY 2014 funds etc.
Nd-no data available

Plans and justification
PMI, and other international donors including Global Fund, will assist the NMCP to achieve universal coverage of ITNs, to maintain that coverage by replacing the ITNs every three years, and support routine distribution through ANC and Expanded Program on Immunization (EPI) clinics. With FY 2015 funding, PMI will continue to support implementation of LLIN mass distribution campaigns, providing 1.5 million nets needed for mass campaigns in 2016. In the six PMI targeted provinces, PMI plans to support routine distribution of free nets for ANCs and pre-school clinics.

A study of routine distribution of mosquito nets was supported with FY 2013 funds at the recommendation of the technical working group. This study collected qualitative data in Bas-Congo and Katanga and used existing data to calculate net coverage rates. Although durability studies were not conducted, qualitative data collected indicated a mean time of use of nets at 1.5 years, due to damage from fires and tears, which would result in increased need for routine distribution if mass campaigns are performed every three years. Using either 1.5 years or 3 years as the average life of a mosquito net, routine distribution is necessary to achieve acceptable coverage rates. In addition to the current routine distribution method (ANC, EPI), the preliminary results of the assessment suggested to plan others continuous distribution (school-based, community health worker-based, marketing social-based, etc.) in order to increase the effectiveness use and availability of ITNs.

The NMCP plans advocacy and resource mobilization with other donors to cover the gaps through 2016. In addition, entomological monitoring and susceptibility assays will be carried out to detect changes in the vector population and to ensure ITNs are effective against the local mosquito populations (see IRS section).

Proposed activities with FY 2015 funding ($17,150,000)
- Procure and distribute 1.5 million LLINs to contribute to the universal coverage replacement campaign in Kinshasa. The funding includes the cost of nets along with household registration, planning, training and supervision and social mobilization/communications. Emphasis will be placed on training and supervising community workers to ensure regular net use. ($6,000,000)
- Support the distribution of 1.5 million LLINs from warehouses to distribution points, storage, supervision, including social mobilization, IEC/BCC, pre- and post- campaign for the mass distribution campaign in Kinshasa. ($3,000,000)
- Procure and deliver to port of entry 1.5 million LLINs for free distribution through routine antenatal and child health clinics in 181 health zones in Kinshasa, Katanga, South Kivu, East Kasai, West Kasai, and Orientale Provinces. ($6,000,000)
- Support the distribution cost for 1.5million LLINs for free distribution through routine services in the 181 target health zones. Funding includes transportation from port to distribution points, storage, and supervision, and reflects the high costs of air shipment in country and is estimated at $1.20 per net. ($1,800,000)
- Support the second year of a pilot of continuous distribution to evaluate possibilities to maintain universal coverage between campaigns. This includes pre- and post-evaluation surveys. ($350,000)

B. Indoor Residual Spraying

NMCP/PMI Objectives
Although IRS is listed in the NMCP's Strategic Plan as one of the vector control methods, a detailed IRS strategy has not been developed for the DRC. Because insecticide-based control methods (LLINs) are being used in the country and knowledge of the malaria vectors is limited, PMI is supporting entomological monitoring in seven sites in five provinces to monitor insecticide resistance and to provide information on mosquito densities and behavior.

Progress since PMI was launched
To date, only one mining company, Tenke Fungurume Mining, conducts yearly IRS as part of their malaria control program targeting approximately 36,000 houses in nine health areas (the subdivision below the health zone level) in the Fungurume Health Zone in Katanga Province. Other gold mining companies are currently discussing a similar activity in Maniema Province with the NMCP.

PMI supported the training of 24 entomologists in mosquito identification, collection techniques, and insecticide susceptibility testing as well as an overview of vector control methods, including personnel from the central level and four provinces. A second training was carried out in June 2013 with 12 participants.

The Global Fund is supporting insecticide resistance monitoring in 11 sites on a one time basis in 2014-2015. The sites have been selected in collaboration with the NMCP and PMI and will add more data to insecticide resistance monitoring in DRC.

PMI/country progress during the last 12 months
In the past year, four entomological monitoring sites were designated for monitoring. These sites were: Kabondo (Orientale), Tshikaji (Kasai Occidental), Lodja (Kasai Oriental), and Kapolowe (Katanga). Sites were visited twice during the year and human landing catches and pyrethrum spray catches were conducted at each visit. *Anopheles gambiaes.l.* was the most commonly collected malaria vector in all sites, with the exception of Lodja, where *Anopheles paludis* was the most commonly collected, although its role in malaria transmission is not known.

Insecticide susceptibility tests were conducted to evaluate the susceptibility of *Anopheles gambiaes.l.* to permethrin, deltamethrin, bendiocarb, and fenitrothion. As shown below, there was no indication of resistance to fenitrothion or bendiocarb, but permethrin resistance was present in all sites (Table 4).

Table 4: Mortality of *Anopheles gambiaes.l.* in WHO tube bioassays

Insecticide (dose)	Family	Kabondo (Orientale)	Tshikaji (Kasaï occidental)	Lodja (Kasaï oriental)	Kapolowe (Katanga)
Fenitrothion (1.0%)	Organophosphate	100	100	100	100
Bendiocarb (1.0%)	Carbamate	100	100	100	100
Deltamethrin (0.05%)	Pyrethroid	100	92	96	95
Permethrin (0.75%)	Pyrethroid	27	45	49	39

Three sites were added to entomological monitoring for FY 2014: Kisangani (Orientale Province), Mikalayi (Kasaï occidental), and Fungurume (Katanga). Kisangani and Mikalayi were added to increase the geographic spread of collection sites and to harmonize entomological monitoring sites with sentinel sites, and Fungurume was added to monitor the effects of the IRS activities on the resistance in mosquitoes.

Plan and justification
PMI will not support IRS with FY 2015 funds in the DRC. The rationale behind this decision is that scaling up distribution of ITNs, which will ensure that people are protected by at least one form of vector control, is more feasible than IRS. The lack of in-country capacity, along with the difficulties in moving throughout the country (often requiring air travel), are major barriers to wide-scale spraying and would substantially increase the cost of this intervention. However, the

resistance monitoring conducted thus far indicates that there is little resistance to organophosphates or carbamates in the DRC, which means that IRS may be considered by the NMCP for future use. Entomological monitoring will continue in seven sites in FY 2015, although the location of the sites may change to ensure even coverage of the country, taking into account the activities of other partners. Monitoring in some sites will be increased to better monitor seasonal factors, secondary malaria vectors, and insecticide resistance.

Proposed activities with FY 2015 funding ($375,000)
- Continue support for entomological monitoring and insecticide resistance assessments at sentinel sites. ($340,000)
- Provide entomological and laboratory equipment, supplies, and reagents for insecticide resistance assays and mosquito identification and processing. ($10,000)
- Provide CDC technical assistance with entomological monitoring in sentinel sites. ($25,000)

C. Malaria in Pregnancy

NMCP/PMI Objectives
The national strategy for prevention and treatment of malaria in pregnancy in the DRC follows the three components recommended by WHO: prevention with an ITN, IPTp, and prompt, effective treatment of cases of malaria in pregnant women. In 2003, MOH adopted IPTp with SP for prevention of the adverse consequences of malaria in pregnant women and their newborns. Women attending ANC pay a standard fee for a prenatal card; this fee includes all ANC services along with the cost of SP and an ITN. Information about the IPTp doses is recorded in the clinic registers. The national guidelines for IPTp were revised in 2013, and now reflect the WHO recommendations for treatment at every ANC visit after the first trimester. The Ministry of Health is in the process of updating its training materials and the new approach has not been fully rolled out at the national level.

The NMCP has identified the following objectives which correspond to the three prongs of the malaria-in-pregnancy program.
- Reduce malaria-specific morbidity and mortality by 50% by 2015
- At least 80% of people at risk sleeping under a ITN
- At least 80% of pregnant women receive IPTp according to national directives
- At least 80% of all patients with malaria receive diagnosis and treatment conforming to national standards at all levels of the health system

In 2013, the DRC also revised its guidelines for the treatment of malaria, including the treatment of cases in pregnant women. The revised guidelines specify the use of quinine in the first trimester, and the first-line ACT in the second and third trimester. However, the guidelines permit the use of quinine for any trimester when ACTs are not readily available. Furthermore, the DRC's policy on folate is that at ANC, pregnant women should receive one combined ferrous sulphate (150 mg) plus folic acid (0.5 mg) a day throughout pregnancy.

Progress since PMI was launched
The most recent DHS shows some evidence of improvement in the coverage of malaria in pregnancy (MIP) interventions in the DRC. Use of antenatal care remained relatively stable since the last survey in 2007, with 88% of women attending antenatal care at least once during their pregnancy. ANC utilization is even higher among urban women (94%), while only slightly less among rural women (86%). In spite of the high levels of ANC attendance, however, IPTp coverage improved only slightly in the past five years. In 2012, 14% of pregnant women received at least two doses of SP from an ANC facility (16% urban, 13% rural). At the same time, use of bed nets among pregnant women increased substantially. In 2012, 60% of all currently pregnant women reported sleeping under a bed net, as compared to only 7% in 2007. When the data are restricted to those pregnant women living in a household possessing an LLIN, 83% of pregnant women reported sleeping under the net. Currently no data are available about adherence to treatment protocols for pregnant women with malaria; however, anecdotal evidence suggests that providers show a preference for quinine as a first-line treatment across all age groups and this is not likely to be different in pregnant women.

Many factors could explain the low coverage of IPTp including frequent stockouts of SP, late ANC attendance, and the fee charged for the ANC consultation. However, since these fees help ensure the functioning of the health facilities and the payment of incentives (primes) for the workers, it may not be in the best interest of the health system to remove them. Because the updated policy on ITPp has not been fully rolled out, many providers still adhere to older, more restrictive guidelines regarding the timing for SP doses. A desk review of MIP guidelines and training materials from the DRC revealed a number of inconsistencies in the guidance between documents produced by the NMCP and documents produced by the Reproductive Health Unit. In general the NMCP documents were more current in terms of the revised WHO recommendations for IPTp, while the training modules and reproductive health guidelines followed older, more restrictive guidance. The latter specify doses at specific times during the pregnancy which is likely an inhibiting factor for providers.

Progress during the last 12 months
PMI supports malaria in pregnancy interventions through its two primary implementing partners, which together cover 138 health zones in 5 provinces. In FY 2013, PMI purchased and distributed 180,689 ITNs for routine ANC and EPI services. In the same timeframe, PMI purchased and distributed 1,123,732 doses of SP for IPTp. According to project registers, approximately 51% of pregnant women in PMI-targeted provinces received at least two doses of SP during their most recent pregnancy. PMI supported training of 3,265 health workers on malaria in pregnancy, including IPTp. A BCC campaign has focused on malaria, including promoting the importance of SP as part of antenatal care.

The NMCP and the Reproductive Health program hold periodic coordination meetings to address issues around implementation of IPTp. Recently, both programs have been working on revising guidance and training materials to reflect the new WHO recommendations. PMI has provided technical support to this process, including sharing the findings of the MIP document review and supporting the effort to harmonize guidance between the two divisions.

The malaria in pregnancy program has been hampered by many of the same supplychain weaknesses that are affecting delivery of ACTs and RDTs, in particular, widespread stockouts of

SP and difficulties in the distribution of ITN through routine channels. PMI commissioned an assessment of the routine net distribution systems to recommend ways to improve this channel. The assessment and recommendations are covered in the ITN section of the MOP. Supply chain issues remain a key priority and FY2015 activities are described in the pharmaceutical management section of the MOP.

Commodity Gap Analysis

Table 5: SP Gap Analysis 2016

Description	2014*	2015	2016
Estimated population in PMI-supported health zones[1]	21,000,000	31,698,005	32,648,948
Estimated pregnant women in PMI-supported health zones	850,000	1,267,920	1,305,958
Total SP needed in doses[2]	1,700,000	3,000,000	3,016,763
SP to be procured by PMI	1,700,000	3,000,000	3,016,763
Gap in SP	0	0	0

*In 2014, PMI covered 138 health zones, but coverage increased in 2015 to 181 health zones. At the same time, DRC had not yet adopted the new IPT guidelines, so SP needs were calculated based on the 2 doses per pregnancy policy that was in effect at the time.
[1] In 181 Health Zones in Kinshasa, Kasai Oriental, Kasai Occidental, Sud Kivu, Katanga, and Orientale in 2016.
[2] Assuming 96% of women attend ANC at least once, and 81% and 54% attend a second and third time respectively.

Plans and justification
To improve the scale-up of MIP interventions in 2015, PMI will focus its support to reduce the stockouts for ITN and SP at routine ANC services and to ensure refresher training to update providers on the WHO recommendations regarding IPTp dosing. Although WHO revised its IPTp recommendations in November 2012, and the DRC adopted the revised recommendations in the spring of 2013, the DRC is still in the process of retraining providers nationwide. PMI will support an integrated cascade training program on the full package of ANC services, and supervision to providers from the province level down to the health zone and health facility level, to ensure that women receive benefits of MIP services.

Because the new recommendations now call for SP at every ANC visit after the first trimester, PMI will increase its procurement of SP to 3 million treatments to ensure an adequate supply of SP to the estimated 1.3 million pregnant women in the 181 health zones. With PMI now covering 181 Health Zones, the MIP program will provide SP to 34% of pregnant women in DRC. PMI will also work on strengthening the supply chain to avoid the stock outs of SP that have hindered this program in the past. Details regarding improvements to the supply chain are covered in the pharmaceutical management section. In addition, PMI will work with the NMCP to ensure that

21

other donors (DFID, World Bank, Global Fund) likewise increase SP procurement to accommodate the new guidelines in the health zones they cover.

PMI will procure 1.5 million ITNs for distribution through routine ANC and EPI services. These nets will cover the need for routine nets in PMI intervention areas, or approximately 1.3 million pregnant women. PMI will also procure RDTs, ACTs, and oral quinine (quantified under the case management section) to ensure that pregnant women have access to appropriate diagnostic and treatment services. BCC activities with both health facility staff and community health workers will include counseling strategies on use of ITN during pregnancy, the importance of early attendance at ANC and obtaining SP at each visit after quickening, and correct diagnosis and treatment of cases of malaria in pregnant women.

Proposed activities with FY 2015 funding ($1,200,000)
With FY2015 funding, PMI will support the following activities for malaria in pregnancy programs:

- Procure 3 million SP treatments to meet the needs of 1.3 million pregnant women in the 181 PMI-targeted health zones areas for the increased number of doses under the new WHO recommendations ($400,000)
- Support the distribution costs for SP, as well as ANC registers, cups, and water filters from the central warehouses to the health facilities ($125,000)
- Procure 1.5 million ITNs for distribution through routine ANC and EPI services to ensure that pregnant women and new mothers and babies are protected by ITNs (costs included in ITN section)
- Procure RDTs, ACTs, and oral quinine for diagnosis and treatment of malaria in pregnant women. (Details and costs for each commodity are described in the case management section).
- Support training and supervision of health workers in the 181 PMI-supported health zones to implement all three elements of the malaria in pregnancy program – ITN, IPTp, and case management for pregnant women. This training will be done through a cascade approach to extend the reach of the program from the central and provincial levels into the health zones and community health workers. ($675,000)

D. Pharmaceutical Management and Case Management
NMCP/PMI Objectives
The national strategy for malaria in the DRC states that, by the end of 2015, 80% of patients with malaria will have access to proper malaria testing and treatment. It also states thatby the end of 2015, 80% of patients with malaria will have access to proper diagnosis and treatment.

Among the 8,266 health centers in the DRC, NMCP aims to train one healthcare worker, maximum of two, per health facility per year, while among the 3,038 iCCM sites, to train two community health workers per site per year. In terms of supervision, the DRC public health authorities envision that each health facility should receive one supervisory visit from the health zone bureau per month, and iCCM sites should receive one supervisory visit per month from the health center with which it is associated. These visits are to be conducted in conjunction with associated stock managers to maintain adequate commodities stocks. The estimates and targets are ambitious, but malaria partners are committed to work toward them. Training of health workers in malaria case management, including the use of RDTs, is to be carried out together with that of prevention of malaria in pregnancy. A seven-day training course is provided to the health zone management team and a five-day course for the chief nurse and/or deputy of the referral health center for each health zone.

In terms of diagnostic training, the DRC aims at training at least two health workers per health facility and two community health workers per iCCM site per year in performing and interpreting RDTs. The National Malaria Control Strategy also includes training of at least one laboratory technician in each one of health facilities aimed at having functioning microscopy at each level of the health system (provincial hospitals, reference health centers, and other key health centers).

According to the national malaria treatment policy in the DRC, all febrile patients should be tested for malaria by either microscopy or RDT. Malaria microscopy is expected to be the primary diagnostic procedure in hospitals and larger health centers, called reference health centers, while RDTs are to be used in smaller health facilities and at the community level. It is expected that each provincial hospital (11 in total), each reference health center (one in each of the 516 health zones), and approximately 4,000 key health centers (out of 8,266 health centers in total) have a functioning microscopy laboratory.

Progress since PMI was launched
In March 2005, MOH adopted AS-AQ for the treatment of uncomplicated malaria and made oral quinine the recommended treatment for patients who failed to respond or had intolerance to AS-AQ. For pregnant women, quinine is the antimalarial of choice in the first trimester of pregnancy while AS-AQ is recommended for the second and third trimesters. Severe cases are managed with parenteral quinine; rectal artesunate can be used as pre-referral treatment of severe cases. In 2012, a forum of experts in antimalarial treatment suggested to include artemether-lumefantrine (AL) as an alternative first-line treatment to AS-AQ, and parenteral artesunate as the treatment of choice for severe malaria. These recommendations were then approved by authorities of MOH in the DRC with a three-year period to phase over to treatment of severe malaria by parenteral artesunate. As of July 2014, PMI focuses its procurement only on AS-AQ as first-line line ACT for the DRC, pending the national rollout of AL.

Training and supervision in case management is supported by PMI and other NMCP partners, but the NMCP staff themselves trains provincial authorities, who then are responsible for training health zone staff. Healthcare workers and community workers are trained by health facility staff. All trainings are done with NMCP-approved training materials. Since beginning of 2013, trainings of healthcare workers in the DRC should include all disease programs and be done according to pre-determined schedules, i.e., stand-alone malaria trainings are not allowed in the DRC. However, the implementation of this policy has been somewhat slow, and malaria trainings are commonly done as stand-alone activities.

Under the leadership of MOH and with the support of USAID, the DRC has been implementing integrated community case management (iCCM) since December 2005, which includes treatment of uncomplicated malaria, pneumonia, diarrhea, and malnutrition. The NMCP has approved case management with RDTs and ACTs at the community level. Currently, a total of 3,038 iCCM sites, covering a population estimated at more than 7 million people, exist in the DRC.

The NMCP and PMI are coordinating efforts with the iCCM Unit of MOH to introduce RDTs in malaria case management at more than 600 iCCM sites out of 1,040 existing iCCM sites in the 5 PMI-supported provinces. In PMI-supported health zones, approximately 1,000 community health workers have been trained and regularly use RDTs and ACTs to treat malaria.

The NMCP has set a coverage target for malaria treatment by 2015 of 80% of patients with a fever being diagnosed and treated according to national guidelines at all levels of the health system; this figure increases to 85% in 2016. According to the preliminary report of the 2013 DHS, 29.2% of children under five were treated with any antimalarial drug and 5.0% had received an ACT. The DHS reports that 14.6% of febrile cases among children under five were treated within 48 hours of fever onset. These figures show progress when compared with the results of previous MICS and DHS, but highlights that provision of timely malaria treatment continues to be one of the biggest challenges in the DRC. These findings can also be related to the change in malaria treatment guidelines, which now recommend laboratory diagnosis before treatment to febrile patients is administered.

Procurement of laboratory diagnostic equipment and supplies is done by individual donors according to the needs of the health zones they support; however, regular maintenance of the microscopes is usually not provided by donors. At health facilities and the community level, the cost for RDT testing is included in the service package fee paid by patients, but microscopy testing usually requires a specific fee to be paid by patients. PMI provides technical assistance directly to the national and provincial public health officers working in malaria diagnosis, in addition to supporting the staff at *Institute National de Reserche Bio-Medicale* (INRB). In PMI-supported health zones, training in RDT use has been integrated into training modules on malaria in pregnancy and malaria case management, while training in microscopy is focused on staff laboratories.

PMI staff in the DRC and PMI partners are in agreement that most of the work related to malaria diagnosis at the peripheral level will be done by those health workers directly involved in case management at health zone level using RDTs. To achieve this, a total of 5,097 healthcare workers were trained by PMI implementing partners in 2013. Of those, 4,087 in the 2,509 PMI-supported health facilities were health facility workers and 1,010 were community-level health workers in the 607 PMI-supported iCCM sites. PMI also supported the production and distribution of 50 bench aids on malaria diagnosis and 350 standard operating procedure guidelines during national and provincial laboratory trainings. PMI implementing partners supported 15 outreach training and supportive supervision visits.

Progress during the last 12 months
Diagnosis
PMI implementing partners working in diagnostics and case management continue to collaborate to make sure the technical content related to RDTs is included in training materials provided to healthcare workers. Considering the reported high percentage of patients who seek care from the

private sector, especially in urban areas, in addition to focusing on the public sector, PMI plans to support an evaluation of testing practices and quality in the private sector in the near future.

In 2013, PMI supported the basic malaria diagnostics refresher training for 21 laboratory technicians from provincial and sub-provincial levels of the 5 PMI focus provinces. PMI expects that this cadre of professionals will support further cascade training and malaria diagnostic quality control and quality assurance programs. Additionally, PMI partners supported the training of 16 microscopists in advanced malaria diagnosis to prepare them for WHO-level accreditation. This figure corresponds to the goal of three reference laboratories at provincial level and the national laboratory at INRB. This would help build strong capacity in malaria diagnosis in the DRC.

Pharmaceutical Management and Treatment
In early 2014, a PMI implementing partner with expertise in drug procurement opened an office in the DRC to support drug forecasting, customs clearance, and distribution of drugs to the provincial warehouses. This partner works closely with other PMI partners involved in case management and provision of care at the health facility and community levels. PMI expects this work to greatly facilitate the pharmaceutical management in the DRC.

In addition, PMI and its partners made progress in distributing case management commodities to health facilities and in communities for iCCM. PMI implementing partners work closely with other NMCP partners to reconcile stocks and demand of drugs and RDTs in order to avoid stockouts, overstock and drug expiration. Distribution and stock management are better coordinated within the different levels of the healthcare system. As a result, stockouts have been reduced.

During the last year, a total of 5,097 health workers were trained in the management of uncomplicated and severe malaria, and also in pre-referral treatment. Of these, the majority (4,087) were health facility health workers, while 1,010 were community-level health workers. Updated figures for number of healthcare workers trained in the whole country were not available at the time this MOP was written. In addition, PMI-supported health zones received at least one supervisory visit from provincial authorities in 2013. As systems to timely and accurately monitor supervisory visits was not in place in the DRC at the time of this operational plan, details on exact number of visits that took place are not currently available.

Gap Analysis
Diagnosis
According to the gap analysis done in May 2014, 6 of the 11 provincial hospitals and 393 of the 516 reference health centers have functioning microscopy laboratories. In addition, the gap analysis showed that approximately 91.9 million, 89.7 million, and 87.5 million RDTs are needed in calendar years 2015, 2016, and 2017, respectively, in the DRC to cover RDT needs in the public sector (Table 6). Those calculations took into account public health system coverage, estimates of number of febrile episodes per year calculated based on morbidity data, and expected percentage of malaria cases that will be indeed confirmed by RDT or microscopy (see details on the estimates in the Case Management section below). The gap analysis plan did not stratify needs by provinces and districts, but considering that 91.9 million RDTs are needed in

2015 to cover the country's total population of 91.8 million people and that PMI's health zones serve approximately 31.7 million people (34.5%) in 181 health zones, a total of 31.7 million RDTs would be needed for the PMI-supported health zones. It is important to mention that PMI is the sole donor for commodities in the health zones it supports.

Table 6: Description of RDT needs in DRC and in PMI-supported areas

Variable	Year		
	2015	**2016**	**2017**
Population	91,777,009	94,530,319	97,366,228
Number of expected febrile cases	106,336,514	116,372,022	119,863,182
Diagnostic testing coverage	80%	85%	90%
Percentage covered by RDTs	85%	90%	100%
Total RDTs needed in DRC	91,874,748	89,664,643	87,500,123
Total RDTs needed in PMI-supported areas (34.5%)	31,696,788	30,934,301	30,187,542

Pharmaceutical Management and Treatment

Table 7 shows the national estimated AS-AQ needs for the public sector in the DRC from the 2014 gap analysis. These calculations were presented as part of the DRC's strategic plan and were calculated by the NMCP and its partners. The number of febrile episodes in the different age groups, utilization rates of public sector facilities, the impact of prevention strategies, and expected positivity rate of malaria tests were all considered in these calculations. It is unclear to what extent these estimates reflect the real needs in the country and the absorptive capacity of the health system. In addition, the estimates do not account for number of ACT treatments needed to 'fill' the drug supply chain and buffer stocks, nor the estimated pipeline. The assumptions made were:

1. Proportion of population by age groups: 0–11 months = 3.49; 1–5 years = 15.41%; 7–13 years = 26.1%; >13 years = 55%.
2. Estimated public health facility utilization rate = 80% (2015) to 85% (2017).
3. Average number of febrile episodes per year for the 0–11 month age group = 1; 1 to 5 year age group = 4; 6 to 13 year age group = 2; >13 year age group = 0.5.
4. Laboratory testing positivity rate: 51%.
5. Available pipeline of drugs.

Table 7: ACTs national estimated needs for the public sector

Drug/Formulation	Patient age group	Year		
		2015	2016	2017
AS-AQ (25/67.5mg) fixed-dose blister-3 tabs	Infants 0–11 months	1,306,831	1,430,163	1,473,068
AS-AQ (50/135mg) fixed-dose blister -3 tabs	Toddlers 1–5 years	23,081,110	25,259,390	26,017,171
AS-AQ (100/270mg) fixed-dose blister -3 tabs	Child 6–13 years	19,546,300	21,390,982	22,032,712
AS-AQ (100/270mg) fixed-dose blister -6 tabs	Adolescents and Adults >13 years	10,297,380	11,269,196	11,607,271
Total need in DRC		54,231,621	59,349,731	61,130,222
Total need in PMI-supported areas		18,655,578	20,416,307	21,028,796

*The population in PMI supported health zones equals approximately 34% of the national population.

PMI recognizes that quantity is low, considering the needs of the health zones which were calculated by the gap analysis. A review of health zones with high consumption rates (the initial 119 health zones supported by the Global Fund) indicates that 5 million RDTs can cover the demand of 12 million people. Although Global Fund-supported health zones are not the same as those supported by PMI, it does give a general sense of ACT consumption. Furthermore, there are relatively high RDT and ACT pipelines in DRC (i.e., almost one year of stock); thus, the country team and NMCP felt that it is appropriate to procure one-third of the projected demand. The DRC is in the initial phase of commodity quantification by consumption, and more accurate data will be available soon.

The assumptions used in the quantification this year have been reviewed by the NMCP and partners during the development of the recent Global Fund concept note. The estimated quantities of ACTs and RDTs are two to three times higher than those estimated last year. A main reason for this escalation is a great increase in the populations size. For FY 2014, the estimated population used was 75 million for the country, whereas for FY 2015, an estimated population of 91.8 million was used. This vast increase in the population estimate reflects the lack of accurate population data available, since the last census in the DRC was conducted nearly 30 years ago. Given the lack of precision on population estimates and associated estimates of need, previous experience on the use of ACTs and RDTs, and the large quantities currently in the pipeline, PMI decided plan conservative procurements to avoid overstocks and expiration of goods. If necessary, an adjustment can be made through reprogramming when more accurate consumption data is available.

Plan and justification
Diagnosis
Both NMCP and INRB understand the critical need to perform supervisory visits and activities related to quality control of diagnostic, especially microscopy at the provincial and health facility levels. Plans for quality control and quality assurance are in discussion with participation of PMI and other partners working in malaria control in the DRC. It is envisioned that a panel of standard malaria slides with different species and parasitemia will be used to evaluate and train microscopists at the different levels of the healthcare system. In addition, a subset of positive and negative slides from diagnostic laboratories will be sent for quality control at their respective upper levels.

Pharmaceutical Management and Treatment Providing effective antimalarial treatment in the DRC is one of the biggest challenges for PMI. In addition to making drugs available at the point of service, attention needs to be devoted to improving utilization rates of public health system in the DRC and healthcare workers compliance with treatment regimens. The low uptake of ACTs in the DRC can be attributed to poor utilization of the public health system, poor acceptability of AS-AQ by both health workers and patients, and the financial incentive to use antimalarials available for purchase. A health facility evaluation is planned for late 2014 to provide comprehensive information on the issues around the provision of care.

Given the low health facility use rate, efforts are being made to expand the coverage of community health workers. These workers should engage in comprehensive malaria control training encompassing routine malaria case management. Partners should be encouraged to develop strategies for both community worker training and supervision. PMI will support the scale-up of iCCM sites with RDTs and ACTs for uncomplicated cases but also rectal artesunate for pre-referral treatments of severe cases in 181 targeted health zones. PMI also plans to procure malaria treatment for use in cases of epidemics and outbreaks.

Proposed activities with FY 2015 funding ($18,125,000)
Diagnosis ($7,612,500)
In FY 2015, PMI will support the strengthening of malaria diagnosis (both microscopy and RDTs) in health facilities and iCCMs in the 181 health zones supported by PMI. The following activities are planned:
- Procure approximately 10 million RDTs for use in the 181 health zones in six provinces to support malaria testing. These RDTs are expected to cover RDT needs in these health zones during implementation of laboratory confirmation at health facilities and at community level. PMI will monitor and be prepared to adjust procurements based on consumption and speed of scale-up. ($6,200,000)
- Supervise and implement a system for quality control and quality assurance of malaria diagnosis, assist in preparation for accreditation of laboratory technicians and provide equipment. This activity will build on the ongoing support by PMI to maintain high-quality microscopy at national and provincial levels. Funding will also allow for the training of trainers at the different levels of the healthcare system. ($500,000)
- Procure microscopes and microscopy kits. PMI will purchase microscopes (at approximately $2,500 each) and microscopy kits and reagents to run 1,000 tests, to support activities in PMI-supported provinces both at provincial and health facility levels.

Exact quantities of these commodities will depend on assessments by PMI implementers, a maximum of 60 microscopes will be purchased and distributed. ($150,000)

- Provide training and supervision to laboratory staff and health workers performing malaria RDTs and also cover distribution costs of RDTs from the provincial warehouses to the 181 PMI-supported health zones. ($750,000)
- Provide technical assistance visit by CDC/Atlanta staff to support activities related to malaria diagnosis and related quality control. ($12,500)

Pharmaceutical Management and Treatment ($10,512,500)

With FY 2015 funding, PMI will support the following activities in the 181 health zones targeted:

- Procure approximately 7.5 million co-formulated AS-AQ treatments for case management of uncomplicated malaria in PMI-supported health zones. ACT usage will be closely monitored to adjust procurement in case of unexpected drug needs or overstocks. PMI will also closely monitor the possible expansion of AL as alternative first-line ACT and consider adjusting purchase orders accordingly. ($4,800,000)
- Procure 62,000 treatments of parenteral artesunate for management of severe malaria. For planning purposes, a treatment was estimated at 300 mg of artesunate (5 ampules), which is sufficient for a 3-day treatment of a 30-kg child (2.4 mg/kg per doses, 4 doses). Final order adjustments will be made based on real needs at time of procurement. ($900,000)
- Procure approximately 600,000 doses of rectal artesunate for pre-referral treatment of malaria. For estimation purposes, a dose is estimated as 100 mg of artesunate, enough for a patient of 10–20 kg. ($100,000)
- Procure 277,000 doses of oral quinine for uncomplicated cases of malaria with intolerance to AS-AQ for cases of treatment failure and for use by pregnant women. For estimation purposes, a treatment is a total course (seven days) for a patient of 20 kg. ($350,000)
- Support in-service training and supervision of facility health workers responsible for the management of both severe and uncomplicated in 181 health zones. This is expected to include a total of 18 provincial laboratory technicians (or three per focus province), 362 health zone laboratory technicians (or two per each 181 health zones), and 3,620 clinicians and community health workers (two health worker per health facility in 181 health zones with 10 health facilities each). ($1,100,000 total)
- Support in-service training and supervision of community health workers responsible for the management of uncomplicated malaria at the community level. This is expected to reach 3,500 clinicians and 2,000 community health workers (one or two community health workers per iCCM site). ($1,000,000 total)
- Support distribution of malaria case management commodities (RDTs and medicines) from provincial warehouses to health zones and health facilities. This is expected to provide support to 181 health zones. ($700,000 total)
- Strengthen the supply chain management for malaria drugs and RDTs, including support to forecasting AS-AQ, SP, and RDT needs, drug inventory management, availability of warehouses at national levels, targeted technical assistance to FEDECAME, forecasting and management of stockouts. This activity will contribute to ongoing support for improving the performance of the supply chain management, mainly monitoring of stock conditions at different levels of the supply chain system (warehousing and at health

facilities), regular monitoring of stocks and usage rates, monitoring of storage conditions (temperature, humidity), and finally tracking of shipments of PMI-procured commodities from CDRs, to health zone bureaus, and health facilities. ($1,050,000)

- Support an in-country office for PMI implementers involved in the delivery of malaria commodities to improve management of shipments, forecasting, obtaining waivers for importation, transportation, etc. ($500,000)
- Provide technical assistance visit by CDC/Atlanta staff to support activities related to case management, in particular, to assist with issues related to training of health providers and community case management of malaria. ($12,500)

E. Monitoring and Evaluation

NMCP/PMI Objectives
The NMCP has identified clear objectives for itself and its partners in the National Strategic Plan 2011-2015. The principal role for the Monitoring and Evaluation unit at the NMCP is to monitor progress towards the objective of reducing malaria-specific morbidity and mortality by 50% by 2015.

The results expected for 2015 are:
- At least 80% of people at risk sleep under a ITN
- At least 80% of households in target zones are covered by IRS
- At least 80% of pregnant women receive IPTp according to national directives
- At least 80% of all patients with malaria receive diagnosis and treatment conforming to national standards at all levels of the health system
- At least 80% of malaria epidemics are controlled according to national standards
- Strengthened national and provincial coordination structures of the NMCP
- Data on indicators of importance to the NMCP are routinely available

Progress since PMI was launched
The DRC is a relatively new PMI country. Early M&E support focused on providing basic technical assistance and training to national-level NMCP staff, and conducting insecticide resistance monitoring as the country began national bednet campaigns. With FY 2012 and FY 2013 funding, PMI partners have worked with the NMCP and other stakeholders to conduct more targeted assessments of community case management, and national M&E systems (in conjunction with the Global Fund) and to build capacity at the NMCP to conduct M&E activities. In FY 2013, PMI provided technical assistance to the NMCP to develop a National Malaria M&E Plan to go along with the National Malaria Strategic Plan, and support to start a technical working group around M&E issues. Since FY 2013, PMI has organized its M&E support around the national plan, providing assistance to the NMCP and its provincial offices, as well as supporting routine monitoring through its implementing partners in country.

Progress during the last 12 months
In the past fiscal year, PMI has provided a wide range of assistance to the NMCP for M&E activities. At the national level, PMI funded a senior M&E advisor, who was hired in July 2013 and sits at the NMCP to provide direct technical assistance and support. In tandem with the placement of the advisor, a national-level workshop on M&E was held in Kinshasa to build

capacity for M&E functions. The workshop brought together staff from NMCP headquarters, provincial NMCP offices, and stakeholder organizations from Kinshasa and the Provincial offices to support the National M&E plan.

To date, the NMCP has collected data through a parallel routine reporting system due to problems with completeness and timeliness of the national health information system (*Système Nationale d'Information Sanitaire, or SNIS*). MOH is currently reconfiguring its health management information system to use the district health information system (DHIS)-2. PMI has supported revisions to the malaria components of that system to ensure that the new DHIS-2 collects a standard set of malaria indicators necessary for program management and reporting. As this system gets rolled out in-country, the parallel NMCP system will be phased out and all routine malaria data will be collected through the HMIS.

PMI was a primary supporter of the 2013 DHS, which was completed in early 2014 with a preliminary report disseminated in May 2014. This survey collected biomarker data for HIV, malaria, and anemia as well as vaccine preventable diseases. The DHS is the first comprehensive survey collecting malaria data since 2007, and will be the first one to provide estimates at the level of the 26 new provinces. Table 8 details the various M&E activities.

A program evaluation of a pilot of the use of rectal artesunate at the community level is currently being implemented. The objective of this study is to test the feasibility and acceptability of introducing rectal artesunate at the community level as a pre-referral treatment. The results are not yet available.

Table 8: Monitoring and Evaluation Activities

Data Source		Calendar Year (2011-2016)					
	Activity	2011	2012	2013	2014	2015	2016
Household Surveys	Demographic and Health Survey			X			
	Malaria Indicator Survey					X	
Entomological Monitoring	Entomological Surveillance		X	X			
	LLIN durability monitoring						X
Malaria Surveillance and Routine System Support	Therapeutic efficacy testing			X			
	M&E training			X	X	X	
	Development of NMCP M&E Plan			X			
	Placement of M&E Advisor at NMCP			X	X	X	X
	Enhanced routine reporting at selected sites				X	X	X
	EUV			X	X	X	X
	Development and maintenance of M&E database at national level			X	X	X	X

Plans and justification
The challenges facing the M&E portion of the National Malaria Control Program are numerous, but at the same time, the DRC offers some unique opportunities for creative approaches to collecting and analyzing data. An assessment of data quality and community case management, as well as a recent joint M&E mission by PMI staff highlighted serious problems with routine data collection at the health facility level. The issues included a lack of reporting forms, difficulties in transmitting data to the next level, and gaps in healthcare worker training on M&E. The MOH is also in the process of revising its routine information system to use the DHIS-2 platform but it has not yet been rolled out to the subnational level. An opportunity exists for PMI to support the development of an M&E system at both the central and sub-national levels to provide essential data for program management at local level while at the same time allowing the NMCP to coordinate and manage on a national level. The existing infectious disease surveillance system in the DRC frequently reports fever epidemics which are often not investigated due to lack of support. PMI plans to provide some limited support to fever outbreak investigation to better understand the extent to which these outbreaks are due to malaria. In addition to supporting the development of capacity of the NMCP staff and the routine information system, PMI plans to support a new MIS survey to provide updated information on coverage and impact in 2015/2016. The timing of the survey complies with PMI's guidance to collect these data every

two years, and will also provide endpoint data for the current National Strategic Plan. Following the survey, PMI has set aside funds for the in-country costs associated with an impact evaluation, which will use the four available rounds of survey data (2007 DHS, 2010 MICS, 2013 DHS, 2015 MIS) to measure the overall impact of malaria control efforts in the DRC.

Proposed activities with FY 2015 funding ($2,062,500)

- Support improved use of data for program management at central level. In order to build M&E capacity within the central NMCP staff, PMI will support targeted technical assistance and training on the use of data for program management. The focus of this activity will be on analyzing program and research data collected by the NMCP and its partners to guide the implementation of the National Malaria Strategy. ($200,000)
- Build M&E capacity at provincial level through training, data analysis, and use. With FY 2015 funding, PMI will provide technical assistance and training to the provincial level NMCP staff to improve the collection, analysis, and use of malaria data. This provincial level assistance will also support improvements in the data collection and aggregation system in selected sites, including coordination among partners working on enhanced routine reporting, roll out of the DHIS-2, and possible SMS data transmission capacity. This activity will also support supervision for data collection, analysis, and quality control. ($200,000)
- Enhanced routine reporting in selected sites. As a complement to the technical assistance provided to the provincial NMCP staff (see above), PMI will support enhanced routine reporting in selected sites (two sites, one per province). This support will include training and supportive supervision for monitoring and reporting activities, printing and distribution of standardized registers and data collection forms, and technical assistance to support data use at the health facility level. In areas with iCCM activities, this activity will also provide similar support to the community health workers in the catchment areas. The funds will be divided between the two service delivery partners in the DRC, each supporting one province for this activity. ($500,000)
- Monitoring and evaluation advisor to the NMCP. PMI will provide continued support to an M&E technical advisor to the NMCP. This individual sits at the NMCP and provides technical expertise to help implement the National M&E Strategy. The advisor also is tasked with building M&E capacity within the NMCP through mentoring and on-the-job training for staff. ($100,000)
- Implementation of 2015/16 MIS. In accordance with PMI M&E guidance, PMI will support a Malaria Indicator Survey in 2015/2016 to collect updated information on intervention coverage as well as biomarkers for anemia and parasitemia. ($500,000)
- Support for fever outbreak investigation. PMI will provide limited funds to support the NMCP in its investigations of fever outbreaks, or unusual increases in malaria case reporting. This support will cover a limited number of field visits of joint teams of experts to conduct the investigations as well as the costs for the collection, transportation and analysis of samples. ($200,000)
- Malaria impact evaluation. The impact evaluation activity is part of a larger portfolio conducted by PMI to document the impact of the scale up of malaria control interventions on morbidity and mortality in PMI focus countries. In FY2015, PMI will provide support to a local research firm to work with PMI impact evaluation staff on data analysis and report writing. ($100,000)

- End-use verification survey (EUV). In order to track the availability of PMI-purchased commodities at the health facility level, PMI will conduct an EUV survey in selected provinces in early 2016. These data will be used to monitor the effectiveness of PMI's efforts to improve the supply chain in the DRC and case management practices at the lowest level of the health system. ($150,000)
- Support training and field data collection to monitor durability of the LLINs distributed in the 2015 mass campaign. These funds will also be used to purchase supplies and equipment to conduct cone bioassays as well as baseline and follow-up laboratory analyses to monitor the insecticide content of the LLINs. ($100,000)
- CDC technical assistance for M&E. ($12,500)

F. Operational Research

As one of the newer PMI countries, the DRC has not yet developed an operational research (OR) portfolio. With FY 2015 funds, PMI proposes to develop a new OR activity to help inform vector control activities. While PMI does not support IRS or other vector control activities in DRC apart from ITNs, other partners and private sector organizations do, and these data will be useful to the NMCP for developing a comprehensive vector control strategy.

Planned activity
- Evaluation of the effects of mass distributions of ITNs on the intensity of resistance in Kinshasa. PMI proposes to conduct an OR study to monitor the effects of a mass-distribution of ITNs on pyrethroid resistance and entomological inoculation rates in Kinshasa province. The proposed study will monitoring insecticide resistance in *Anopheles gambiae*, the primary malaria vector present in Kinshasa, over the course of a year during which a mass campaign is planned. Resistance will be monitored using CDC bottle bioassays, including the intensity bioassay, and resistance mechanisms will be determined using standard molecular methods. The results will be used to inform vector control activities. ($100,000)

G. Behavior Change Communication
NMCP/PMI Objectives
The country's BCC strategy, designed with PMI's support in 2012, aims to increase awareness among target populations for increased use of malaria prevention and control measures through culturally sound communication activities. The NMCP uses a sociological approach to behavior change, which targets populations most affected by malaria, collaborates with key actors who influence behavior (traditional, opinion, and religious leaders), and takes into account the social context which dictates behavior. The BCC strategy combines different channels of communication (television, radio, multimedia, and interpersonal communication), social mobilization, advocacy, and capacity building of stakeholders. Innovative approaches to social and behavior change communication, many of which were developed by PMI-supported activities, are promoted under this strategy to ensure greater impact and efficacy of activities. At the national level, the National Health Communications Program coordinates, establishes norms and provides guidance on BCC activities across the various health programs, as well as review provincial level communication work plans to oversee BCC strategies in each of the 11 provinces. There is also a Communications Task Force, led by the National Health Communications Program with support from USAID health partners, to coordinate health

messages and activities between the various bilateral and multilateral health programs. PMI partners are active in this task force, as well as the BCC focal point of the NMCP.

Progress since PMI was launched
Since 2011, PMI has supported BCC activities in targeted health zones in line with the national strategy, to promote use of malaria preventive measures and treatment services. The package of malaria services has been supported with an array of BCC activities that include community sensitization around routine preventive services for malaria in pregnancy and immunization to deliver IPTp and LLINs, as well as community mobilization via the community health promoters (*relais promotionnels*) to ensure correct and timely use of ITNs as well as to improve care-seeking behavior. Since August of 2012, with the support of a PMI partner, PMI has strengthened the capacity of the NMCP to coordinate BCC activities among partners and stakeholders, and develop effective and quality materials for BCC interventions. More specifically, a PMI implementing partner trained NMCP central and provincial coordinators on BCC in the provinces of Oriental, Katanga, South Kivu, and Eastern and Western Kasais. It has sponsored MOH participants to attend a malariology course, and facilitated the SBCC module.

PMI supported the update of the National BCC strategy, as well as the dissemination of the NMCP malaria and prevention treatment guidelines. Finally, PMI has supported the production of promotional tools for nets distribution, a comic book to support the students at their schools, and supported a malaria day campaign in targeted provinces.

Progress during the past 12 months
During the past year, PMI supported the production of BCC materials and other promotional items such as job aids, message guides, banners and posters. A BCC workshop was conducted at the national level as a collaboration effort between PMI partners and the NMCP to produce a communication plan for a PMI-supported project and to identify key messages on malaria intervention issues, including the use of ITNs, care-seeking behavior, case management, and prevention of malaria in pregnancy. A total of 850 job aids were distributed, and 267 healthcare workers were trained in BCC.

Various BCC approaches were taken to deliver BCC messages in Eastern and Western Kasai, South Kivu, and Katanga, including broadcasting messages through community radio, short message service (SMS) messages, mini campaigns, website blogs, and interpersonal communication. PMI-supported projects sent 51,907 SMS, distributed 2000 posters on AS-AQ dosage, distributed 2000 job aids, and 3,350 counseling cards. Community outreach workers performed 45,400 home visits and the Health Area Committees (CODESA) held about 102,000 awareness sessions on malaria. The education through listening approach through the Champion Community reached about 400,000 people in 4,300 sessions. 16,800 group talks with community level CBOs and NGOs were held, as well as 1,250 information sessions on malaria during church gatherings.

The PMI-sponsored "Students Against Malaria" BCC campaign conducted in 2014 targeted pupils aged 10-14 years old using a comic book as educational material. Each student was tasked to discuss what they had learned about malaria with10 people at their school, neighborhood, or family. A total of 21,299 people were reached with BCC community outreach. Additionally,

PMI supported the development of an educational guide for military, police, and religious leaders to promote health behaviors for malaria treatment and prevention.

Messages disseminated include the importance of sleeping under LLINs, seeking treatment at health facilities at the onset of fever, and adherence to the full regimen of prescribed treatment. Messages also emphasized the use of LLINs among children less than five years of age and pregnant women as well as the advantage for pregnant women in attending ANC services for IPTp uptake. PMI will ensure that appropriate tools are in place to monitor BCC activities and the impact of messages on population behavior. BCC activities will be evaluated under planned end of project and mid-term evaluations

Plans and justification
In FY 2015, PMI will continue to support implementation of the national communication strategy in PMI-supported health zones. BCC activities will be focused on raising awareness of health workers, religious leaders, community health workers, community groups, school students, and other malaria stakeholders on the importance of malaria prevention and treatment. BCC messages will be integrated into BCC activities throughout the health portfolio to leverage the effectiveness and reach of interventions. PMI will also engage government officials, donors, parliamentarians, and private sector for increased attention to malaria, mobilize resources, and greater coordination of activities.

In compliance with PMI BCC guidance, BCC support will continue to utilize local effective communication channels that are culturally sound and familiar to the communities and target populations. BCC activities in the DRC will also address the following keys issues on the provider and patient, while supporting advocacy for policies that address other systemic determinants.

- Increase the use of ACTs as a first-line treatment for malaria: Only 29.2% of fevers reported among children under five were treated with antimalarials (14.6% within 24 hours of symptoms onset), and only 5% were treated with ACT. Despite the policy, quinine remains the main anti-malarial used to self-treat fever, and is widely prescribed by health workers even when ACT is available in healthcare facilities. BCC efforts towards this end will address both provider practices and patient knowledge and compliance with treatment.
- Increase the coverage of IPTp for prevention of malaria in pregnancy: More than 88% of pregnant women attend ANC at least once in DRC and 79% make two visits. In spite of this, only 14.3% of pregnant women received two doses of SP during ANC visits. DRC is currently revising its national protocols for IPTp and the BCC activities will help to inform healthcare workers and create demand among pregnant women.
- Stimulate the use of ITN among targeted risk groups: While the use of ITN has shown improvement major gaps remain. Only 55.9% of children less than five years of age and 60.3% of pregnant women sleep under an ITN. A recent assessment on ITN use showed a major drop in ITN use between campaigns. BCC activities will complement the ongoing universal coverage campaigns, routine distribution of nets at health facilities, as well as explore social marketing as a means to increase ITN use.

- Promote the acceptability of three new commodities: RDTs for malaria diagnosis, injectable artesunate for treatment of severe cases, and rectal artesunate for pre-referral treatment of severe case at the community level.
- Explore the barriers to access and uptake of malaria prevention and treatment approaches in order to inform BCC activities across the PMI portfolio in DRC.
- Enhance coordination and on BCC activities at all levels of the health system. Coordinating BCC activities remains a challenge, from the operational level, to the provincial and national level.

Proposed activities with FY 2015 funding ($1,325,000):
- Support BCC activities to raise awareness among the population on ownership and use of ITNs, mainly by the vulnerable group, during routine distribution. PMI will support sensitization at antenatal care and immunization clinics by healthcare providers; advocacy meetings with community leaders; family outreach by community health workers; community and small group discussions; explore social marketing of ITNs, SMS; television and radio spots, posters. ($400,000)
- Support the cost of promoting the use of malaria treatment commodities and services. PMI will promote changes in provider behavior to use AS-AQ as the first-line treatment of malaria; improve patient knowledge of malaria services through sensitization at antenatal care and immunization clinics by healthcare providers; advocacy meetings with community leaders; family outreach by community health workers; community and small group discussions; SMS; television and radio spots, posters. The cultural determinants will be explored to better understand health worker behavior, and BCC interventions will be developed to counter inappropriate provider behavior. ($560,000)
- BCC training for community health workers to promote MIP interventions, including ITN use, IPTp, and treatment-seeking behavior for suspected malaria along with general messages on the importance of antenatal care 181 health zones in 6 provinces. Activities at the community level and interpersonal communication will also promote the malaria in pregnancy interventions. ($315,000)
- Support NMCP advocacy activities in order to increase political will and mobilize GDRC resources (both human and monetary), engage greater involvement with government, donors, parliamentarians, and the private sector through meetings, workshops, and development of materials and media campaigns. ($50,000)

H. Health Systems Strengthening/Capacity Building

NMCP/PMI Objectives
The 2011-2015 the DRC National Health Development Plan clearly states the objective of improving the health of the population through poverty reduction efforts. More specifically, the revised malaria strategic plan (2013-2015) aims to achieve this objective by several means: (a) reinforcing participative planning at all levels, including at the community level; (b) building service providers' capacity at all levels; (c) supplying health facilities with malaria commodities; (d) improving human resources management; (e) supporting research; (f) reinforcing behavior change communication for malaria prevention and control; (g) reinforcing surveillance, monitoring and evaluation, and (h) reinforcing program coordination. Despite the high-level commitment to the strategic plan, the capacity of the health system in general and the NMCP in

particular need to be improved to ensure better coordination at national and sub-national levels. MOH has shown a clear commitment to integrate health services at health facility and community levels to improve access to healthcare services.

Progress since PMI was launched
In support of the GDRC's efforts to conduct reforms of the health system geared toward increasing Congolese's' access to healthcare, PMI continues to expand the provision of the minimum malaria package of services to under-served health zones. From the 138 health zones in FY 2012, PMI is currently expanding to 43 additional health zones, most of which are located in the Katanga Province. In the GDRC's current decentralization reform, the Katanga Province, with almost 10 million of people, will be divided into four provinces each with its Regional Health Office (DPS). In line with the Mission's Country Development and Cooperation Strategy (CDCS), Katanga province is a major focus province for USG development assistance. This province will also host 59 PMI health zones, representing almost one-third of the total of 181 PMI-supported health zones. Countrywide, PMI-supported health zones will represent 35% of the 516 health zones.

PMI has also supported a series of capacity building activities over the past three years, including training in entomology, the Field Epidemiology and Laboratory Training Program (FELTP), malaria in pregnancy, malariology, case management, and social behavior change communication. Technicians and health workers from the national, provincial, and community levels attended these trainings.

Progress during the past 12 months
Given the multiple challenges the supply chain and the drugs distribution system are facing, the DRC, PMI, and PEPFAR partners conducted a joint trip in November 2013 to assess the logistic management information system (LMIS) and provide recommendations to improve the production of accurate data for sound forecasting, procurement and distribution of commodities to healthcare delivery points. Discussion is underway between the mission, MOH and those involved partners to implement the recommendations in the near future. As an interim solution to reduce delays in processing PMI commodities shipped to the country and facilitate diligent distribution, PMI has approved one additional supply chain management partner to open an office in the DRC.

During the past year, PMI supported the strengthening of the NMCP's management capacity through assigning a monitoring and evaluation specialist to the program. This support has provided more visibility to the monitoring and evaluation unit of the program and will contribute to reinforce the coordination of data collection, analysis, processing and use for decision-making. The PMI-sponsored M&E specialist is primarily in charge of assisting the NMCP coordinate the implementation of its M&E plan, which is an integral part of the revised malaria national strategic plan. PMI has also supported the NMCP to improve program coordination. As a result, PMI's partner supported 100% of malaria task force quarterly meetings (4/4) planned at the national level and 85% of those planned at the provincial level (17/20).

To enable the NMCP face the challenges in coordinating the increasing flow of funds from multiple donors in malaria control, PMI, in collaboration with DFID, sponsored an assessment of the organizational capabilities of the NMCP. The concerted selection process led by MOH has been completed in May 2013 with the selection of a regional consulting firm. PMI, DFID, and other partners will support the NMCP implement the recommendations of the assessment.

As planned in the previous MOPs, PMI has supported advisors embedded in the provincial malaria control teams. As of writing, all the five provincial advisors have been recruited, posted, and are fully operational.

Capacity building
USAID and officials from the GDRC have increasingly emphasized the need for capacity building activities to ensure ownership and sustainability of the malaria control program. PMI supports the USAID/ DRC Mission's CDCS to support the country not only to build strong institutions to boost its development, but also to strengthen the capacity of citizens to participate in development process. Donors, such as DFID, are also planning to support the NMCP in the next few years to build capacity within the program and at all levels of the health system in order to better implement and coordinate the program.

Progress during the past 12 months
During the past 12 months, PMI resources have been extensively invested in supporting various training activities designed to assist the NMCP and the DRC health system achieve its overarching goal of reducing mortality and morbidity due to malaria. In addition to training and supervising health workers at the health facility and community levels, PMI has also supported many malaria-related training activities. The following table provides an overview of the training support funded by PMI during the past 12 months.

Table 9: Overview of trainings provided under PMI during the last 12 months

#	Description of Training activities	Target	Number of persons trained in FY 13	Comments
1	Field Epidemiology and Laboratory Training	20	20	Participants from 4 provinces (Bandundu, Katanga, Kasai and Bas-Congo)
2	Malariology training		36	7 were trained in the past two years
3	Entomology	12	12	At national and provincial levels
4	Case Management-Diagnosis	7,613	5,134	Health providers at health zone level
5	Case Management-ACT	7,576	5,097	Health providers at health zone level
6	Monitoring and Evaluation	27	27	NMCP staff at the central and provincial levels
7	ITNs and IPTp	3,148	3,265	At provincial level
8	Journalists trained on malaria prevention and treatment	26	26	National and provincial level
9	Behavior Change Communication	20	19	National and provincial levels

As planned in previous years' MOPs, PMI has completed the recruitment for five malaria advisors' positions designed to reinforce the management and technical capabilities of provincial malaria control program units. This represents a significant input to the program as these advisors are considered integral part of provincial malaria program teams.

Plans and justification
Placing an emphasis on building technical leadership and managerial capacity at all levels of the health system is important for successful implementation, monitoring, and evaluation of the malaria control program. Ultimately, the return on investments in capacity building will be seen in their impact on child mortality in the DRC. PMI will continue its strong focus on building technical and managerial capacity for malaria prevention and control at all levels of the health system. More specifically, PMI will continue to support the NMCP to improve the quality, completeness, and timeliness of malaria-specific data reporting from health facilities and to strengthen staff skills in data analysis, interpretation, and reporting of findings, both from routine supervision and other data sources such as HMIS, DHS, and MIS.

To enable the NMCP to take responsibility and improve coordination of the malaria program in the current context of decentralization, PMI will support the implementation of the recommendations that will result from the organizational capacity assessment. Like other provinces, PMI-supported provinces are slated to undergo decentralization reform whereby each of them will be divided into three or four provinces. Thus, PMI's support will reflect such reform and more investment will be needed to support the new DPSs that will be created and within which a NMCP unit will also be created. PMI will continue emphasizing technical training and technical assistance in the focused-provinces by building the capacity of provincial malaria control team, within the regional health offices.

Training and technical assistance will mainly target the supply chain management system in order to improve commodity forecasting, quantification and distribution to avoid recurrent stock-outs of drugs. Support to the supply chain will include increasing storage capacity and improving storage conditions of regional warehouses (CDRs).

Proposed activities with FY 2015 funding ($1,435,000)
PMI will support the following capacity building and health system strengthening efforts. The selected capacity building activities will complement other donors' support such as the Global Fund and DFID's plan to provide a package of trainings to the NMCP.

- Continue support to the country coordination efforts as well as national and provincial malaria task force teams, to help address the NMCP's desire to improve coordination of government, donor and civil society malaria program activities and resources. This activity includes support to Task Force meetings at the national as well as at the provincial level and annual program review. ($100,000)
- Support targeted malariology training course with the Kinshasa School of Public Health. Nine people will be sponsored at national and provincial levels to attend the international or local training courses organized by the WHO. ($100,000)
- Support national and provincial-level staff training on communication and monitoring and evaluation. This activity consists of supporting in-country training sessions for national and provincial levels staff on behavior change communication and in monitoring evaluation. The two training activities which are also organized at the international level will enable attendance of an increased number of participants. ($200,000)
- Support Field Epidemiology and Laboratory Training Program (FELTP*)*. This activity will focus on building the country's capacity in malaria epidemiology, particularly early detection, management and response plan for malaria epidemics. ($150,000)
- Support the costs for five province-based malaria advisors. ($250,000)
- Support the NMCP to develop the next five-year strategic plan, including its M&E and BCC plans. ($50,000)
- Collaborate with PEPFAR to strengthen the supply chain management by improving commodities storage conditions at the provincial level to support proper disposal and delivery of malaria commodities in one province. ($250,000)
- Support the recommendations of the NMCP organizational assessment. This activity will be conducted in collaboration with other donors at the national and provincial levels. Support will include provision of small work equipment to improve work conditions of target provincial NMCP (office spaces, computer and internet connectivity for reporting). (335,000)

I. Staffing and Administration

Two health professionals serve as Resident Advisors to oversee the PMI in the DRC, one representing CDC and one representing USAID. In addition, five Foreign Service Nationals (FSNs) will work as part of the PMI team: three PMI staff, and two FSNs who will work on the cross-cutting issues of supply chain management and logistics and community case management. All PMI staff members are part of a single inter-agency team led by the USAID Mission Director. The PMI team shares responsibility for development and implementation of PMI strategies and work plans, coordination with national authorities, managing collaborating agencies and supervising day-to-day activities. Candidates for resident advisor positions (whether initial hires or replacements) will be evaluated and/or interviewed jointly by USAID and CDC, and both agencies will be involved in hiring decisions, with the final decision made by the individual agency.

PMI professional staff work together to oversee all technical and administrative aspects of the PMI, including finalizing details of the project design, implementing malaria prevention and treatment activities, monitoring and evaluation of outcomes and impact, reporting of results, and providing guidance to PMI partners.

The PMI lead in country is the USAID Mission Director. The two PMI resident advisors, one from USAID and one from CDC, report to the Senior USAID Health Officer for day-to-day leadership, and work together as a part of a single interagency team. The technical expertise housed in Atlanta and Washington guides PMI programmatic efforts and thus overall technical guidance for both RAs falls to the PMI staff in Atlanta and Washington. Since CDC resident advisors are CDC employees (CDC USDD—38), responsibility for completing official performance reviews lies with the CDC Country Director who is expected to rely upon input from PMI staff across the two agencies that work closely day in and day out with the CDC RA and thus best positioned to comment on the RA's performance.

The two PMI resident advisors are based within the USAID health office and are expected to spend approximately half their time sitting with and providing technical assistance to the national malaria control programs and partners.

Locally-hired staff to support PMI activities either in Ministries or in USAID will be approved by the USAID Mission Director. Because of the need to adhere to specific country policies and USAID accounting regulations, any transfer of PMI funds directly to Ministries or host governments will need to be approved by the USAID Mission Director and Controller, in addition to the USG Global Malaria Coordinator.

Proposed activities for FY 2015 funding ($3,087,500)
- Salaries and support costs of one USAID PSC, one CDC direct hire, and three USAID FSNs, two FSNs jointly funded with other mission funding, including equipment, ICASS, other Mission taxes and fees, and other associated expenses including the TBD Bilateral baseline survey by a third party ($3,087,500)

Table 1
President's Malaria Initiative – DRC
FY 2015 Budget Breakdown by Partner

Partner	Geographical Area	Activity	Budget ($)	%
TBD Bilateral	113 health zones in 5 provinces	Transport of malaria commodities from Provincial Warehouse to service delivery points in 113 health zones, training and supervision of facility- and community-based health workers and lab technicians in IPTp, CM, IMCI, BCC. Support NMCP capacity building at provincial level by hiring one provincial malaria officer	$4,810,000	11%
PMI Expansion	68 health zones in 5 provinces	Transport of malaria commodities from Provincial Warehouse to service delivery points in 68 health zones, training and supervision of facility- and community-based health workers and lab technicians in IPTp, CM, IMCI, BCC. Support NMCP capacity building at provincial level by hiring provincial malaria officers in four provinces	$4,100,000	9%
TBD SCM	National & Provincial	Procurement of LLINs, ACTs, RDTs, severe malaria drugs, pre-referral treatment, SP, oral quinine, laboratory supplies, operational costs of commodities, and supply chain management	$19,400,000	43%
UNICEF	Kinshasa Province	Conduct province wide mass distribution of LLIN, including household installation	$9,000,000	20%
MalariaCare	National & Provincial	Continue building the capacity of the country and NMCP at central and provincial level on malaria diagnosis and quality assurance of testing	$500,000	1%
TBD IEC/BCC	National & Provincial	1) Support country coordination mechanism at the national and selected provincial levels (malaria task force committees) 2) Support targeted malariology training course	$250,000	1%

The Demographic and Health Survey Programs	National & Provincial	Provide technical assistance to the NMCP and partners in planning, developing questionnaires, implementing and conducting data analysis for the Malaria Indicator Survey.	$500,000	1%
TBD M&E	National & Provincial	Support of NMCP at central and provincial-levels to collect, analyze, disseminate data and decision making. Support the NMCP to develop the next five-year strategic plan, including its M&E and BCC plans.	$500,000	1%
MSH/SIAPS	National and five provinces: West Kasai, East Kasai, Katanga, South Kivu and Orientale	Strengthening of supply chain management including conducting end use verification	$1,200,000	3%
TBD with INRB sub-grants	National & Provincial	1) Continue building the capacity of the country and NMCP at central and provincial level, National Biomedical Research Institute for species identification and insecticide resistance monitoring in 7 sentinel sites of PMI-supported provinces; 2) Support the evaluation of *Anopheles paludis* as a malaria vector in the region of Sankuru- Western Kasai; 3) Study of infectivity, insecticide resistance, and seasonal effects on malaria vectors in Kinshasa	$440,000	1%
TBD-ITN	1-2 provinces / 3 health zones (1 rural, 1 peri-urban and 1 urban)	1) Second Year of Pilot continuous distribution, following NetWorks Assessment; 2) Conduct LLIN durability study per PMI guidance	$450,000	1.0%
TBD	National	PMI Impact Evaluation	$100,000	0.2%
TBD	National	Support the NMCP to develop the next five-year strategic plan, including its M&E and BCC plans	$50,000	0.1%
TBD SCM	National	Collaborate with PEPFAR in strengthening supply management by improving a provincial warehouse	$250,000	0.6%

CDC IAA	National and five provinces: West Kasai, East Kasai, Katanga, South Kivu and Orientale	1) Targeted technical assistance in LLIN, case management and M&E; 2) Support to the Field Epidemiology Laboratory Training Program (FELTP); 3) Full support for the CDC resident advisor	$892,500	2%
USAID	National & Provincial	Staffing, administrative and management related costs	$2,417,500	5%
Total			**$45,000,000**	**100%**

Table 2
President's Malaria Initiative - DRC
Planned Obligations for (FY 2015)

Proposed Activity	Mechanism	Budget		Geographical area	Description
		Total $	Commodity $		
PREVENTIVE ACTIVITIES					
Insecticide Treated Nets					
Procure long-lasting insecticide treated bed nets (LLINs) for mass campaigns	UNICEF	6,000,000	6,000,000	Kinshasa Province	Contribute to universal coverage of LLINs in Kinshasa Province through provision of 1.5 million nets. This includes the cost of net delivery to Kinshasa. ($4/net).
Distribution costs for long-lasting insecticide treated bed nets (LLINs) for mass campaigns	UNICEF	3,000,000		Kinshasa Province	Support the distribution of 1.5 million LLINs from warehouses to distribution points, storage, supervision, including social mobilization, IEC/BCC, pre- and post-campaign. ($2/net)
Procure LLINs for routine distribution through ANC and EPI clinics	TBD SCM	6,000,000	6,000,000	181 health zones in 6 provinces (Kinshasa, West Kasai, East Kasai, South Kivu, Katanga and Orientale)	Provide 1.5 million LLINs to support routine services; $4/net.
Distribution costs for routine LLINs from port to distribution points, storage and supervision	TBD Bilateral	1,200,000		113 health zones in 5 provinces (Kinshasa, West Kasai, East Kasai, South Kivu, and Katanga)	Support the distribution cost for 1,000,000 LLINs @ $1.2/net for routine services in target health zones. Also storage and supervision are included in this activity.

Activity	Mechanism			Location	Description
	PMI-Expansion	600,000		68 health zones in 5 provinces (West Kasai, East Kasai, South Kivu, Katanga and Orientale)	Support the distribution cost for 500,000 LLINs @ $1.2/net for routine services in target health zones. Also storage and supervision are included in this activity.
Second year of pilot continuous distribution following NetWorks Assessment	TBD - ITN	350,000	150,000	3 health zones (1 rural, 1 peri-urban and 1 urban)	Maintain universal coverage between campaigns in addition to routine distribution. This includes pre- and post-evaluation survey.
SUBTOTAL ITNs		**17,150,000**	**12,150,000**		
INDOOR RESIDUAL SPRAYING					
Insecticide resistance monitoring	TBD with INRB sub-grants	340,000	0	5 provinces (7 sites)	Continue support for species identification and insecticide resistance monitoring and sentinel sites in supported provinces.
Supplies for entomological monitoring	CDC/IAA	10,000	0	National + five provinces	Provide collection equipment and supplies and reagents for insecticide resistance assays and mosquito identification.
Technical assistance for entomological monitoring	CDC/IAA	25,000	0	National	Assist INRB in establishing functioning entomological monitoring sites and other related activities.
SUBTOTAL IRS		**375,000**	**0**		
MALARIA IN PREGNANCY					
Procurement of SP	TBD SCM	400,000	400,000	181 health zones in 6 provinces (Kinshasa, West Kasai, East Kasai, South Kivu, Katanga and	Procure 3 million SP treatments for 1.3 million expected pregnant women in the targeted health

Activity	Funding Source	Amount	Subtotal	Location	Description
					zones.
					Orientale)
Distribution costs for SP from CDRs to distribution points.	TBD Bilateral	75,000		113 health zones in 5 provinces	Support the distribution cost of 1.7 million SP for routine services in target health zones, including ANC registers, cups, water, etc. to all pregnant women
	PMI-Expansion	50,000		68 health zones in 5 provinces	Support the distribution cost of 1.3 million SP for routine services in target health zones, including ANC registers, cups, water, etc. to all pregnant women
Training and supervision of facility and community-based health workers in malaria in pregnancy.	TBD Bilateral	425,000		113 health zones in 5 provinces	Train health workers with initial or refresher courses in targeted zones in 5 provinces. This includes health workers from both public and private sectors and supervision.
	PMI-Expansion	250,000		68 health zones in 5 provinces	
SUBTOTAL MIP		**1,200,000**	**400,000**		
SUBTOTAL PREVENTIVE		**18,865,000**	**12,550,000**		
CASE MANAGEMENT					
Diagnosis					
Procure of RDTs	TBD SCM	6,200,000	6,200,000	181 health zones in 6 provinces (Kinshasa, West Kasai, East Kasai, South Kivu, Katanga and Orientale)	Procure and distribute about 10 million RDTs to support malaria diagnosis in 181 health zones in 6 provinces, in compliance with NMCP case management guidelines. ($0.63/RDT)
Support reference laboratories at national and	MalariaCare with INRB sub-grants	500,000		National, provincial and selected referral hospitals	Supervise and implement system of quality control in national and provincial reference laboratories,

Activity	Description	Geographic Area	Funding Source	Amount	Amount
provincial levels for microscopy and RDTs training of trainers	as well as selected reference hospitals; assist in preparation for accreditation and provide equipment.				
Support to provincial laboratories at provincial and health facility levels with microscopy commodities	Purchase of microscopes and reagent kits at reference laboratories at the national and provincial levels, as well as selected reference hospitals.	National, provincial and selected referral hospitals	TBD SCM	150,000	150,000
Train and supervise laboratory technicians and other health workers to perform RDTs at the health zone level and to distribute RDTs at the health zones and health facility levels.		113 health zones in 5 provinces	TBD Bilateral	400,000	
	Support training activities to strengthen capacity of laboratory technicians and other health workers to perform RDTs at the health zone and health facility levels.	68 health zones in 5 provinces	PMI-Expansion	350,000	
Technical assistance	Support capacity building for diagnostics.	National	CDC IAA	12,500	
SUBTOTAL -- Diagnosis				**7,612,500**	**6,350,000**
TREATMENT AND PHARMACEUTICAL MANAGEMENT					
Procurement of ACTs	Procure 7.5 million ACTs treatments for uncomplicated malaria, both for health facilities and community case	181 health zones in 6 provinces (Kinshasa, West Kasai, East Kasai, South Kivu, Katanga and Orientale)	TBD SCM	4,800,000	4,800,000

Activity	Funding			Location	Description
					management (7 million treatments @$0.7/treatment) to fill gaps and prevent stock-outs.
Procurement of drugs and supplies for treatment of severe malaria	TBD SCM	900,000	900,000	181 health zones in 6 provinces (Kinshasa, West Kasai, East Kasai, South Kivu, Katanga and Orientale)	Procure 62,000 treatments of injectable artesunate each @ $14.30 each for treatment of severe malaria
Procurement of drugs for pre-referral treatment of malaria	TBD SCM	100,000	100,000	181 health zones in 6 provinces (Kinshasa, West Kasai, East Kasai, South Kivu, Katanga and Orientale)	Procure 600,000 doses of rectal artesunate for pre-referral treatment of malaria.
Procurement of oral quinine	TBD SCM	350,000	350,000	181 health zones in 6 provinces (Kinshasa, West Kasai, East Kasai, South Kivu, Katanga and Orientale)	Procure 277,000 doses of oral quinine for cases of ACT intolerance and pregnant women in the first trimester.
Training and supervision of facility-based health workers trained in case management	TBD Bilateral PMI-Expansion	700,000 400,000		113 health zones in 5 provinces 68 health zones in 5 provinces	Support training and supervision activities to strengthen facility-based health workers in 181 health zones in 6 provinces to manage malaria cases in an integrated fashion per NMCP guidelines.
Build and maintain capacity to provide community case management services	TBD Bilateral PMI-Expansion	600,000 400,000		113 health zones in 5 provinces 68 health zones in 5 provinces	Identify, train, equip and supervise community health workers to provide community case management services.
Distribution costs for all case management (diagnosis and treatment) related commodities from provincial	TBD Bilateral PMI-Expansion	400,000 300,000		113 health zones in 5 provinces 68 health zones in 5 provinces	Support the distribution and storage costs of all case management-related commodities including diagnostic commodities for routine services in target health zones.

Activity	Mechanism				Location	Description
warehouse (CDRs) to distribution points						
Strengthen the supply chain management for drugs and RDTs including End use verification	SIAPS	1,050,000			181 health zones in 6 provinces	Contribute to ongoing SIAPS support activities for supply chain management and addressing stockouts, testing storage conditions (temperature, humidity) for drugs and RDTs. Support monitoring and tracking of PMI commodities from CDRs and health zones to delivery points. 10 staff, 2 per province.
Support for operational costs related to commodities in country	TBD SCM	500,000			Six provinces	Support proper delivery of malaria commodities in the DRC including coordination of commodity shipments and delivery in provincial drug warehouses.
Technical assistance	CDC IAA	12,500	10,512,500		National	Support capacity building for case management.
SUBTOTAL - Treatment & Pharmaceutical Management			**10,512,500**	**6,150,000**		
SUBTOTAL CASE MANAGEMENT			**18,125,000**	**12,500,000**		
MONITORING AND EVALUATION						
Support better use of data for program management at the	TBD - M&E	200,000			National	Support training on data analysis and use for program management, supervision, coordination.

Category	Activity	Funding Source	Amount	Location	Description
central level	Build M&E capacity at provincial level through training, data analysis, and use	TBD - M&E	200,000	Two provinces (TBD)	Build M&E capacity and improve systems at the provincial level by supporting provincial level training in M&E, piloting of improved data collection and aggregation system in selected sites, and supervision for data collection, analysis, quality control, and use for program decision-making This also includes printing standardized reporting forms.
	Expansion of enhanced routine reporting in selected health facilities (centers of excellence) through training, supervision, data collection, aggregation, and use.	TBD Bilateral	250,000	Two provinces (TBD)	Training and supervision of central and provincial-level NMCP staff in data collection, analysis, quality control and use for program decision making; including printing forms, training and supervision at provincial level.
		PMI-Expansion	250,000		
	Continued support for an M&E Liaison with TA to NMCP	TBD - M&E	100,000	National	Support of an M&E professional to work at the National Malaria Control Program Division to coordinate and conduct M&E activities.
	Implementation of 2015 Malaria Indicator Survey	The Demographic and Health Surveys	500,000	National	Provide technical assistance to the NMCP and partners in planning, developing questionnaires, implementing

	Program			and conducting data analysis for the MIS.
Malaria surveillance and outbreak investigation	PMI-Expansion	National	200,000	Support malaria outbreak investigation (or unusual increase in malaria) including field visits of joint teams of experts and fees for collection, transportation and analysis of samples.
Malaria impact evaluation	TBD	National	100,000	PMI impact evaluation.
EUV	SIAPS	National	150,000	End use verification survey.
LLIN durability	TBD - ITN	1-2 provinces	100,000	Conduct LLIN durability study per PMI guidance.
Technical assistance	CDC IAA	National	12,500	Assist national M&E planning, support capacity building for M&E
SUBTOTAL M&E			**2,062,500**	**0**
OPERATIONS RESEARCH				
Entomological	TBD with INRB sub-grants	Kinshasa province	100,000	Study of infectivity, insecticide resistance, and seasonal effects on malaria vectors in Kinshasa.
SUBTOTAL OR			**100,000**	**0**
BEHAVIOR CHANGE COMMUNICATION				
IEC/BCC for routine distribution of	TBD Bilateral	113 health zones in 5 provinces	250,000	Support IEC/BCC activities to raise awareness among the population on ownership and use

Activity	Funding	Amount		Location	Description
LLIN	PMI-Expansion	150,000		68 health zones in 5 provinces	of bed nets, mainly for vulnerable groups.
IEC/BCC related to case management	TBD Bilateral	260,000		113 health zones in 5 provinces	Support the cost of promoting use of malaria treatment commodities and services through IEC/BCC activities.
	PMI-Expansion	300,000		68 health zones in 5 provinces	IEC-BCC training for community health workers on MIP interventions, including bednet use, IPTp, and treatment-seeking behavior for suspected malaria along with general messages on the importance of antenatal care in 181 health zones in 6 provinces.
IEC-BCC-related to malaria in pregnancy, cascading elements for community health workers and communities.	TBD Bilateral	190,000		113 health zones in 5 provinces	
	PMI-Expansion	125,000		68 health zones in 5 provinces	
Support NMCP advocacy activities	TBD IEC/BCC	50,000		National	As part of resources mobilization, engage government, donors, parliamentarians and private sector including mining companies through meetings, workshops and development of materials and media campaigns.
SUBTOTAL - BCC		**1,465,000**	**0**		
HEALTH SYSTEM STRENGTHENING/CAPACITY BUILDING					
Continue to support country coordination mechanisms at the national and provincial levels	TBD IEC/BCC	100,000		National & Provincial	Support multi-partner National Malaria Task Force at the central and provincial levels, including meetings, report dissemination, support to technical assistance for coordination, annual review.

54

Activity	Funding Source	Amount	Location	Description
Support targeted malariology training course	TBD IEC/BCC	100,000	National & Provincial	Support the training of nine health experts at the national and the provincial levels to attend the international or local malariology training courses organized by WHO in the DRC.
Support national-level training workshop for provincial-level staff on communication and malaria control	PMI-Expansion	200,000	National & Provincial	Support in-country training sessions at the national and provincial levels staff in communication (IEC/BCC) and in monitoring and evaluation. The two trainings which are also organized at the international level will enable an increased number of participants in the DRC.
Support Field Epidemiology and Laboratory training Program	CDC IAA	150,000	National	Support Field Epidemiology and Laboratory Training Program with (FELTP) malaria focus.
Support to NMCP capacity building at provincial level	TBD Bilateral	60,000	South Kivu	Strengthen the capacity of the NMCP at the provincial level in strategic planning, policies, guidelines and M&E planning through locally-recruited Malaria Advisers.
	PMI-Expansion	190,000	West Kasai, East Kasai, Katanga and Orientale	
Support to NMCP capacity building at the national level	TBD	50,000	National	Support the NMCP to develop the next five-year strategic plan, including its M&E and BCC plans.
Collaborate with PEPFAR in strengthening supply management by	TBD	250,000	National	Support proper delivery of malaria commodities in DRC.

improving a provincial warehouse					
Support NMCP organizational assessment recommendation to improve program management and coordination	In coordination with DFID, support organizational assessment and follow-on team building and restructuring of the NMCP at central and provincial levels.	PMI-Expansion	National	335,000	
SUBTOTAL - HSS/CB				**1,435,000**	**0**
IN-COUNTRY STAFF AND ADMINISTRATIVE COST					
In-country staff and administrative expenses	One Resident Advisor, two Malaria Program Specialists, one (30%) Malaria Commodities and Logistics Specialist, one (30%) Community Case Management Specialist, one Administrative Assistant, Program Design and Learning.	USAID	National	2,417,500	
	One Resident Advisor.	CDC IAA	National	670,000	
SUBTOTAL - In-Country Staffing				**3,087,500**	
GRAND TOTAL				**45,000,000**	**25,050,000**